POPULAR POETRY
IN SOVIET RUSSIA

BY

GEORGE Z. PATRICK

UNIVERSITY OF CALIFORNIA PRESS
BERKELEY, CALIFORNIA
1929

CONTENTS

PAGE

PREFACE.. vii

CHAPTER I

DEVELOPMENT OF PEASANT POETRY... 1

THE SPIRIT OF CONTEMPORARY PEASANT POETRY................................. 12

CHAPTER II

ATTITUDE OF THE PEASANT POETS TOWARD THE REVOLUTION............. 16

CHAPTER III

THE RELIGIOUS ELEMENT IN PEASANT POETRY..................................... 27

CHAPTER IV

LOVE OF RUSSIA IN PEASANT POETRY.. 43

CHAPTER V

LOVE OF NATURE IN PEASANT POETRY.. 56

CHAPTER VI

THE ATTITUDE OF THE PEASANT POETS TOWARD THE CITY................. 67

CHAPTER VII

THE ORIGIN AND DEVELOPMENT OF PROLETARIAN POETRY IN RUSSIA 78

CHAPTER VIII

ATTITUDE OF THE PROLETARIAN POETS TOWARD THE REVOLUTION.... 95

CHAPTER IX

Communism, World Revolution, Atheism.. 109

CHAPTER X

"The Iron Messiah".. 127

CHAPTER XI

The Proletarian Hymn to the City.. 142

CHAPTER XII

Conclusion.. 152

APPENDIX

Selected Poems and Biographical Notes.. 157

Index of Authors and Poems.. 287

PREFACE

This book attempts to reveal the new spirit of the Russian peasantry and the Russian city proletariat through the medium of their post-revolutionary poetry. The hundreds of volumes that have been published since 1917 in this country and in England with the aim of interpreting Russia have said little about the literary productions of the last decade. Yet literature, and above all poetry, which is the soul of literature, is the best means of penetrating into the soul of a people. Through poetry better than through anything else one can understand the intimate thoughts, the deep yearnings, and the motive forces at work in a people's life. The peasant and proletarian poetry, being the truest expression of the dominant emotions, ideals, and aspirations of the Russian masses, will enable us to comprehend their state of mind and those springs of thought that underlie and reveal their outlook on life and action.

Of art, in the conventional sense of the word, there is not much in the Russian popular poetry. The reader will find in the verses of both peasants and proletarians much of the crudeness belonging to writers who lack culture and refinement. As tillers of the soil and as factory workers, these poets know little of science, of philosophy, or of the fine arts. They are uneducated men, straight from the people, whose observation is at first hand. They have no subtlety of phrase, no artistic perfection of form, but in speaking from heart to heart they move us deeply; consequently their poetry is significant and worthy of attention. Every one who wishes to know Russia as a whole, or to study the different phases of the Russian Revolution, should be familiar with it. No other texts written in Russia or outside Russia will give so perfect an insight into the mind of the Russian masses, into the emotional background of the Russian Revolution, as the peasant and proletarian poetry.

In order not to encumber my text with too many quotations I have decided to relegate to an Appendix a number of poems of the most outstanding peasant and proletarian poets, together with short biographical notes.

Chapters IV and X of this book are reproductions, with some slight alterations and additions, of articles contributed to the *Slavonic Review,* London, whose editors have kindly granted permission to reproduce that material here. The remainder of the volume has not been hitherto published.

I wish to express my warm appreciation and thanks to Professor George Rapall Noyes, of the University of California, as well as to Mrs. Florence Noyes, for their advice, encouragement, and help. They have both given most generously of their time, and their many constructive suggestions have added greatly to the value of this volume. I am also indebted to David Wight Prall, Associate Professor of Philosophy, University of California, for the help he has given me in the early stages of my work. In the preparation of this book I have also had the continuous encouragement of Professor Sir Bernard Pares, K.B.E., Director of the School of Slavonic Studies, University of London, and Editor of the *Slavonic Review,* London. I am glad of this opportunity to express to him here my deep gratitude. G. Z. P.

BERKELEY, CALIFORNIA,
December, 1928.

I

DEVELOPMENT OF PEASANT POETRY

> Sad are the songs that I sing,
> Sad as autumn's bleak days.
> They are the patter of rain
> And the wind's dreary moan;
> They are my heart's bitter sobs
> And my breast's heavy groan. . . . .
> —*Surikov.*

Those familiar with Russian life and literature were not amazed at the appearance of a large group of peasant poets immediately after the Revolution of 1917. These poets had had their precursors, and their advent on the literary field was to be expected. The development of peasant poetry in Russia was a historical necessity. It was bound to come, as "the lyric cry" of the many millions of human beings who, kept in servitude and deprived of their freedom for centuries, were longing for liberty and for a better life. During the reign of Nicholas I, whose autocratic and oppressive régime culminated in the disastrous Crimean war, the life of every class in Russia became a tragic poem. The peasants, who formed the most important social class, and who had been heretofore almost inarticulate, began to raise their voice in literature, and soon new currents made themselves felt in Russian poetry.

Thus, in the thirties of the nineteenth century, there appeared on the literary horizon Alexey Koltsov (1808–1842), who took as the subject of his poetry the realities of peasant life. The son of a cattle-dealer, and brought up on the steppes, Koltsov, in his rather short poetical career, made the peasant language an instrument of art, and sang in it the joys and sorrows of the tillers of the soil, whom he knew so well.

In a period when only the upper classes of Russia took a real interest in literature and supplied nearly all the poets and prose writers, the appearance of a peasant poet was of particular importance. Up to that time the peasant had been considered by most of the aristocrats as an animal, or even worse, as an object without any feelings or affections. Koltsov went to the root of peasant life, approached his subject in its most intimate aspects, and showed that the peasant was not a beast, but a man whose emotions are identical with those of all human beings. This fact had been felt somewhat vaguely and half-unconsciously by a few intellectuals before the appearance of Koltsov; but only a poet from the peasant class could make it be felt by all with emphatic clearness. By his poetry, by his songs, every word of which sets itself to music and dances to its own tune, Koltsov revealed to Russian society that the peasant has an esthetic soul; that in spite of his ignorance and lack of education the peasant is capable of creating poetical images and symbols which might be envied by any cultured poet. Koltsov, as the first poet of his class, also presented the spiritual qualities of the peasantry. He showed them capable of great endurance and great faith, and free from any spirit of rebellion. The conditions of the peasant's life were such that he might easily have become embittered, and of course there were cases of individual protest among the serfs. But the poetry of Koltsov bears witness to the fact that the characteristic trait of the peasantry in those days—and this is also true of later times—was not revolt, but humility.

This prominent feature in the peasant's soul was strikingly portrayed in subsequent years by the two greatest of the Russian novelists, Turgenev (1818–1883) and Tolstoy (1828–1910), who had such a perfect knowledge of the Russian heart. In Turgenev's *Sportsman Sketches* and in Tolstoy's *Polikushka* we find realistic descriptions of peasant life before the emancipation. These are sad stories, and there is much suffering and anguish in them. Their chief characteristic, however, is not to be found in their gloomy pictures of the peasant's wretched life, but in their emphasis on his humble resignation to it, his calm acceptance of his fate.

Koltsov's poetry had already revealed the same truth, Koltsov, while singing songs full of lightness, of gaiety, of good spirits, compelled the Russian Intellectuals to stand in amazement before the spirit of endurance of the peasantry. He was the first to make it clear that the peasant's ability to suffer prevails over his ability to rebel: that is the primary importance of Koltsov's work.

Painting from actual experience, he revealed to us the mystery of the peasant's many-sided life, always depen-

dent as it is upon soil and weather. He sang in pure and
simple words the hope which the tiller of the soil has in his
heart.

> With a silent prayer
> Will I plough and sow.
> Bring me, O Lord,
> Bread, my riches!

Simple as this utterance is, it tells the whole tale of the
peasant's aspiration.

Merrily following the plough and the harrow, Koltsov
discovered to the Russians all the secrets of agricultural
life, of the harvest, the fields, the streams, the larks, the
blackbirds, and the nightingales.

> Charmed by a rose's radiance bright,
> The nightingale sings day and night.
> Yet silently hears the rose his song. . . . .

Koltsov's sun is always glad and smiling, and his harvest
field never cheerless.

> Like God's guest, on all sides,
> Smiles the glad sun;
> The light breeze passes o'er the fields,
> Rustling the golden corn
> In a shining pathway. . . . .

The poet's imagination was fired by the wild beauty of
the steppes, which had also excited the enthusiasm of the
great Russian realist Gogol (1809–1852). Particularly
charming are Koltsov's little pictures of the steppe in
spring-time:

> All enameled with flowers,
> Quivering from the flight of birds,
> Which, night and day,
> Sing marvelous songs. . . . .

All his poems lap us in the caressing air of rural Russia at its best and make us feel that we are really in possession of the charm and the secret of the steppe. Nothing in nature escapes Koltsov's eye and, following the traditions of the Russian anonymous folk-ballads, the poet often animates the phenomena of nature. The clouds, lightning, thunder, fire, water—all are alive and breathe. "Winter is coming, clad in a fur coat," the river "chatters," and the dense wood is at times sad.

> Why, dense wood,
> Art thou lost in thought?
> Why with sorrowful sadness
> Is covered thy brow? . . . .

Koltsov was naturally aware of the great sufferings of the serfs, and now and then, as in the poem, "A Bitter Lot," we hear his sharp cry of anguish. Grief then weighs heavily on his heart. But in spite of his sorrow, he went on "singing songs with the nightingales," believing that, after all, it was not worth while to lose oneself in despair and disillusionment.

The essence of Koltsov's poetry is absolute simplicity, and of this quality the Russian peasant is possessed. Communion with nature and contemplation induce deep emotion in the peasant; and of this feeling, so profoundly national, so traditionally marked in the treasure-house of Russian folklore, and so humanly appealing, Koltsov is an excellent illustration. His poetry is the finest symphony of rural life. It is no wonder, therefore, that many of his poems and songs have been set to music by the best Russian composers.

Following Koltsov came Taras Shevchenko (1814–1861), a native of the Ukraine, who had himself been a serf for twenty-four years, and who sang in the so-called Little Russian dialect the tragedy of serfdom. This peasant bard, who spent about two-thirds of his life in bondage and prison, is now seen to be the greatest glory of Ukranian poetry. And his is a glory that no Russian finds it hard to recognize. The works of Shevchenko are divided into Songs, Ballads, Poems, Plays, and Novels. He deals boldly with very different subjects and makes his appeal to readers of varying tastes: to the artistic temperament in the Songs, to the patriotic in the Ballads, to the political in the Poems, to the sentimental in the Plays and Novels. But through all the changes of subject Shevchenko never fails to make us aware of his real sympathies, which are always for the oppressed serfs. To emphasize the miserable conditions of the Cossack-ploughmen, the poet pictures in striking contrast the old and the new Ukraine, the one "free and bright," the other "enslaved and weeping."

> There was a time—the Cossacks lived
> And feasted on their fields.
> They feasted merrily, achieved
> Glory at their free will,
> And that has passed! . . . .
>
> There was a time—the merry dance
> Chased grief from out the Ukraine. . . . .

But now "all that is no more," now "the ploughing Cossack sighs to be free again." And we hear the poet pouring out his just anger and sorrow over the "dear and weeping Ukraine'' that he had so loved. We hear him condemning the evil institution of serfdom extended to his native land in 1793 by Catherine the Great, and protesting against it as only he could protest, with all his might. Most of Shevchenko's songs are songs of hate; his verses incite to revolt. This spirit engendered by his long and bitter sufferings was never tamed.

> Bondage is hateful, drear and bad;
> To live free and asleep, more hateful still. . . . .

The natural conclusion, which the poet could not express on account of the censorship, was clear enough: in order to throw off the yoke of slavery and oppression all, even those who were free, should act, should revolt. His own early experiences and afflictions left permanent traces upon the serf-bard.

> My youth of toil, tears, silent pain
> Long past, before me reappears! . . . .
> . . . .
> My youth comes back—then I despair! . . . .

And in his despair he continues to express his fierce anger at the monstrous régime which was continually thwarting genius as Shevchenko knew in his own case, and as he saw in the case of those around him.

Other Russian poets, of greater fame than Shevchenko, wrote powerful verse in behalf of the peasants and the serfs. The most famous among these was Nikolay Nekrassov (1821–1877), in whom all those who sympathized with ''the people'' found their most eloquent voice. But the difference between Shevchenko and Nekrassov is that the former came from the people, while the latter, and other cultured poets as well, with all their enthusiasm for the people belonged to a quite different social sphere. Shevchenko could and really did reflect the inner life of the serfs, of which he was both a witness and a participant, better and more truly than did Nekrassov.

Shevchenko was not a great thinker and he seldom, if ever, walked side by side with his contemporaries, the Slavophiles and the Westerners, in the great highway of human thought; but no poet of prerevolutionary Russia expresses so boldly the spirit of revolt against slavery.

During the period from the emancipation of the serfs in 1861 to the Russian revolution of 1917, the tone and spirit of peasant poetry undergo a change. Owing to the nascent struggle of industrialism with agrarianism, and the compelling attraction which began to lure many peasants from the village to the city, the joyful tone of agricultural life as expressed by Koltsov disappears completely in the poetry of Nikitin (1824–1861), Surikov (1811–1880), Drozhin (1848———), and others. One misses also the forceful spirit of protest to be found in Shevchenko's poetry. Nikitin, the son of a tradesman, had a broader intellectual outlook than his two predecessors, but he lacked their energy and their power to waken an intense emotional thrill. The tone of his poetry is mournful and melancholy, and it sets all his thoughts in a sort of twilight. His favorite themes were his own tragic fate and the fate of the "poor people" with whom the circumstances of his life brought him into daily contact. The years of his youth spent in poverty, sadness, and loneliness were always present in his mind. In 1860, just a year before he died, Nikitin wrote about those sad days: "I should be glad to forget you, but then nothing would be left to remind me of my sad life." In this respect, as in many others, Nikitin is quite different from Koltsov who, in his sorrow, never uttered a cry of despair. The poems which Koltsov wrote at the end of his life show that strength, faith and hope swallowed up all his personal grief.

> Suffering did not bend me,
> Proudly bore 1 fate's blows,
> I preserved desires in my soul,
> Strength in body, fire in heart!
>
> In my soul there was strength,
> In my heart blood,
> My tomb is under the cross,
> My love on the cross.

Nikitin's personal sorrow left no strength in his soul or body, no fire in his heart. "I grew old while I was still young," said Nikitin of himself, when he was only thirty, and in later years, throughout his whole life in fact, his heart continued to ache, and the poet went on:

> Only sorrow remains, only sorrow grows.

With Nikitin peasant poetry underwent a great transformation. The bright and pleasant colors of Koltsov became dark and gloomy, gaiety vanished, the lightness turned into levity, the music became forced and elaborate; the instrument was warped.

Surikov, Drozhin, and all the other peasant poets that followed Nikitin lacked originality and offered nothing absolutely new either in their themes or in their treatment of them. In half-weeping tones they constantly sang of the "bitter fate of the poor peasants" whose material welfare had indeed improved very little since their emancipation. The great agrarian reform of 1861, while completely changing the legal position of the peasants, was not thorough enough to do away with their wretched economic condition. The land allotments which they received were too small to give them the necessary means of subsistence, while the taxes and dues which they had to pay for the land were high and burdensome. The peasant poets found no poetic strength to protest against such conditions. With a kind of elemental and childlike simplicity they sang of calm submission and patient resignation to the tragic fate of peasant life.

> O my fate,
> Fate of the poor,
> How hard and bitter,
> How hard and joyless
> Thou art! . . . .
> O my sorrow, my bitter sorrow,
> Such must be my fate. . . . .
>
> —*Surikov.*

Even the new and vigorous tone brought into Russian literature in 1892 by Maxim Gorky (1869–) did not affect the melancholy notes of the peasant bards. To them the sharp tone of Gorky's vagabonds was very unpleasant and even disgusting. In Gorky's heroes, who regarded the agriculturist as an object of contempt, the peasant poets could see nothing but posing. Nor did the short-lived revolution of 1905 change the spirit of the "Surikovtsy." Like most of their contemporaries, they were soon completely disillusioned as to the "liberties" granted by Nikolas II. Schooled by adversity, they saw clearly Russian life as it actually was. The situation filled them with unaffected sorrow, and melancholy became more and more the keynote of their verses. But melancholy is a very monotonous thing; and, fine as are many of the verses of Nikitin, Surikov, Drozhin, and their followers, their poetry as a whole is wearisome, lifeless, and languid.

II

THE SPIRIT OF CONTEMPORARY PEASANT POETRY

Away with sorrow's frown!
Now I am joyous and bold. . . . .
                                    —*Oreshin.*

The March revolution of 1917 not only uprooted and overturned the dynasty of the Romanovs, but it also brought about the November revolution which, in its turn, has changed to a considerable extent the whole life of Russia. Since Bolshevism came into power there has been a complete change in Russian social laws, in the relation of individual to individual, and of the individual to the state. There has been a change, and there will probably be further changes in the rôles of the social classes, in their ideals, mentality, feelings, and moods. There has been an entire break-up of old ethical and esthetic forms, and of everything that seemed to our fathers and forefathers unchangeably fixed. It is not an exaggeration to say that with the revolution of November, 1917, Russia passed from an old to a new era. But a new age demands new poets, whose inspiration is derived directly from the great social movements of their time, who have absorbed the new ideas growing up around them, and whose voices are in harmony with the spirit of the new era. The voices of the prerevolutionary poets, peasant and cultured, seem out of tune with the new social currents, with the new rhythm and motives of contemporary Russian life. And so the revolution brought forth its own poets.

These new poets could no longer be satisfied with the poetic utterances of their predecessors: in their poems they have struck indeed quite a different note. The revolution has inspired them with a new faith in the future, and they now feel, quite in the spirit of the new age, that they have risen high above the despondency of the past and its patient abandonment to fate. No longer is their poetry filled with despair and lamentation; dark colors have given place to brightness, courage, determination, and hope.

> Away with sorrow's frown!
> Now I am joyous and bold:
> Over the abysses, the chasms and waterfalls
> The Angel of Freedom has flown.
>
> Over each hut, the bird of gladness!
> Over each hut, the fiery dream!
> And the wind kisses the red lips
> Of the night's pale face.
>
> *—Oreshin.*
>
> Enough of rotting and moaning
> And soaring praise of the hideous.
> Washed and wiped off is thy pitch,
> Resuscitated Russia mine!
>
> *—Essenin.*

All the poets address themselves to Russia and their fellow-poets in the most encouraging words:

Enough of suffering and bending!
Rise, beloved, in all your height.
Behold, the brightest dawn
Has dissolved the darkness of night.
To be always sorrowful is not for you,
To you there is a bright road . . . .

—*Shiryavets-Abramov.*

Come out from the small, untidy huts
Into the open, ye sons of the people! . . . .
See how bright the fire is burning . . . .
Russia calls upon us to build a new life,
To fight for the peasant's cause . . . .
Enough of weariness and laziness.
Awake from the age-long sleep,
Ye ploughmen, my brothers.

—*Kuzmichev.*

Never before, not even after the stormy uprisings of 1905, had the Russian people heard such spirited songs. Immediately after the social disturbances of 1905 a few young popular poets, animated by the faith which possessed their souls, had begun to show signs of enthusiasm in their verses. As they became aware however of the dangers which were threatening and which almost killed the new-born child of liberty, the enthusiastic tone soon disappeared. But after the November revolution of 1917, when complete victory over the "dark forces" was won, the outburst of exaltation became greater than ever. Hence the songs of triumph. The popular poets seem to proclaim with the sound of trumpets that a new life is beginning, and that the former slaves henceforth constitute a part of it. They boldly and joyfully adjust the beat of their verse to the beat of the new era, and in contrast to the former laments

> O my sorrow, my little sorrow,
> Such must be my fate . . . .

they sing:

> Not with the moans of my fathers
> Shall my song resound;
> But with the force of thunder
> It shall fly over the earth.
> Not as an inarticulate slave
> Continually cursing his life,
> But as a free eagle
> Will I sing my song.
> —*Kluyev.*

> With a clamor I'll sing to the people my song,
> The song of freedom, the song of strength.
> I'll disperse the sorrow and send it along
> With the friendly clouds and turbulent winds . . . .
> The people will awake, and take a deep breath,
> And unfurl its mighty wings.
> —*Tsarkov-Vysokovsky.*

Thus, whereas the voice of the popular poets, from the emancipation of the serfs in 1861 to the Revolution of 1917, became ever more lifeless and languid, more despondent and disheartened, the voice of contemporary peasant poets has been growing ever more resonant and vigorous, more bold and forceful. Their joyful spirit freshens and quickens the blood till life takes on brighter colors than it ever had before.

Chapter II

ATTITUDE OF THE PEASANT POETS TOWARD THE REVOLUTION

> For land and freedom, for earned bread
> We march in arms to meet our foes!
> Upon us enough they did tread!
> Rush on to fight, to blows!
>
>   —*Kluyev.*

All the peasant poets enthusiastically welcomed the revolution of 1917, which was but the natural outcome of the economic and political strife that had been going on in Russia for many decades. As true representatives of their class, the peasant bards were permeated with the conviction that the time had come when all the arable land would at last belong to those who till it. They earnestly believed that with the revolution there would come an end to the era of masters and slaves, of oppressors and oppressed. The peasants have always had a firm and settled conviction that the agrarian reform of 1861 brought only another form of serfdom, though much of the arable land passed then into their hands. They were persuaded that when they should get rid of the land-owners there would be no more "land-hunger," no more poverty, no more suffering. In 1917, while the war was still going on, they were told, and they naïvely believed, that as soon as the peasant soldiers stopped fighting the Germans and Austrians and concluded peace with all their enemies, Russia would have plenty of food and plenty of everything else. There was no end to explicit promises to the peasantry, which, if carried out, would have made the Russian land a real Eden. Hence when the November revolution came it struck a sympathetic chord in the souls of the peasant poets, and they sang of it with great enthusiasm and joy.

> Since Russia has waked from her sleep,
> She will feast richly and merrily . . . .
> Ye who are young, come all
> To our feast,—there will be plenty for all.
> We are now tsars and magicians
> Of intoxicating songs, of resonant chords,
> Ye who are young, come all.
>
> —*Praskunin.*

> Do not wake those who are asleep,
> The dawn has blushed with a crimson deep,
> March ye all who trust the men of toil,
> Our heritage we are destined to foil.
>
>> The moon reigns o'er the dark,
>> O'er the day lords the sun,
>> With scarlet banners our march we start.
>
> Too long we were a trade for the tyrants,
> Lulled to sleep by the clergy and merchants,
> For the nobility, like cattle we were herded;
> Grandfather and father with a knout were murdered.
>
>> The moon reigns o'er the dark,
>> O'er the day lords the sun,
>> With scarlet banners our march we start.

The age of parasites is past;
Workmen and peasants perished fast;
Their huts were not thatched,
The cot and the field in their need were matched.

The moon reigns o'er the dark,
O'er the day lords the sun,
With scarlet banners our march we start.

Now the new sun is rising
Over the great land of the peasants;
Into our little window it is bravely shining,
The hale and singing spring is with us.

The moon reigns o'er the dark,
O'er the day lords the sun,
With scarlet banners our march we start.

—*Deyev-Khomyakovsky.*

These songs were indeed "intoxicating," for they reached and touched to its very depth the heart of the peasants. "Herded like cattle" for many centuries, always living in utter poverty, in "unthatched huts," the peasants were drunk with joy that "the age of parasites is past." Such songs could not but revive their spirit and hope, and make them dream of building a "new edifice" for a better life. It is no wonder that the ecstacy is general; the chains of hardship are being broken, and the peasants, the great force of the country, are rising to fight for land and freedom.

Yesterday's slaves break the chains,
Yesterday's pariahs forge the swords.
. . . .
Friends, our day is hot and red,
Our world a tempestuous ocean.

To the fight rises the peasant,
The giant of work and thought.
—*Praskunin.*

For dreams there is no room in my bosom,
My soul is on wings of gold.
Holy Russia is my bride
And I am her beloved groom.
—*Oreshin.*

Spread out, O eagle's wings,
Toll, tocsin, and ye the thunders rumble,—
The fetters of oppression are but broken links
And the prison of life doth crumble!
Vast are the Black Sea plains,
Turbulent is Volga, and rich with gold is Ural.
Go, vanish into air, the bloody block and chains,
The prison and iniquitous tribunal!

For land and freedom, for earned bread
We march in arms to meet our foes!
Upon us enough they did tread!
Rush on to fight, to blows!

Over Russia there passed a fiery pheasant,
Kindling vehement wrath in the heart . . . .
Virgin-Mother,—our little earth Thou art—
Bear Thou the free bread for the peasant!
The rumors of old and the dreams came true,
Svyatogor[1] is the people, and now wide awake,
Honey is on the loaves of a rustic cake,
And the tablecloth shows a bright pattern too.

For land and freedom, for earned bread
We march in arms to meet our foes!
Upon us enough they did tread!
Rush on to fight, to blows!
—*Kluyev.*

---

[1] A giant of Russian folklore; the reference to his awakening is taken from a popular ballad.

> The peasants with fiery ensigns
> March in file through the villages.
> Land and freedom are finer than gold,
> Land and freedom is our motto.
>
> —*Oreshin.*

"Land and freedom" was indeed the main aspiration, the long yearning of the peasants. As far back as 1773 hundreds of them had joined in the rebellion of Pugachev, and had demanded "land and freedom." For nearly a hundred and fifty years, they had renewed this demand again and again. But the higher classes of society so haughty, so shortsighted, and so bitterly hostile to the principles of democracy, neglected to meet the peasants' hope, and the land question was never settled satisfactorily. Whatever good may be said of the Tsars, history bears witness that their policy was always directed toward the achievement of their own glory rather than toward the glory of Russia as mirrored in the wishes of its people. This egoistic attitude of the various Russian rulers was the main cause of the revolt of their people. Engaged from childhood in a life and death struggle with misery, hardly able to keep body and soul together, the peasants saw their only salvation in the land. And in the volcanic eruption of November, 1917, when the hesitating Provisional government was overthrown, the peasantry grasped the opportunity and realized at last their profound and everlasting wish. They finally became the owners of all the arable land. In that moment of exaltation, their dim eyes began to shine, their heads became intoxicated, and they did not even mind calling themselves Bolsheviks.

After the long, dark night,
After sad tales, anxious dreams,
Our eyes are shining
Brighter than blue cornflowers.
                              —*Praskunin.*

The sky is like a church bell,
The moon like a tongue,
O mother, country mine,
I am a Bolshevik.
                              —*Essenin.*

Soon after, however, when they learned what Bolshevism stood for, the peasant poets showed that they were not at all interested in it. It could not have been otherwise, for the Bolshevik government embarked upon schemes which found no response in the sentiment of the great masses of the people. Russian peasants have never taken a keen interest in politics, and until just recently they have never bothered themselves much about the affairs of the state. Still less interest have they shown in foreign affairs: the international aims and dreams of the Bolsheviks could have no appeal for them. Their poetry tells us that their enthusiasm and unaffected joy, all their "merry feasts," "golden wings," and "shining eyes" are not the expression of political freedom or a universal commonwealth. These mean very little, if anything, to the Russian peasants. Moreover, they found out immediately after the November revolution that, so far as political freedom was concerned, bolshevist Russia was no better, if it was not actually worse, than the Russia of Nicholas II. The jubilant strain of unhesitating welcome of the new order of things, expressed in contemporary peasant poetry, is due primarily and exclusively to the settlement of the agrarian question. The Russian peasant moves in quite a different world from that of the urban worker, in a world as far removed from scientific socialism as is the planet of Mars from the earth. This is difficult to bring home to the average foreigner, to whom the ideas of the Russian peasants have always been, and still are, a sealed book. But it is perfectly clear to everyone who knows their psychology. As soon as they had got the long coveted land, the peasants were satisfied, overwhelmed with joy, and everything around them seemed to share in their happiness.

> How can one refrain from praying and singing
> When everything around us sings?
> The forest and the meadow, the stream and the birds,
> All are smiling like friends.
>
> —*Klychkov.*

The history and the way of life of the Russian peasants show clearly that they have always been fanatically attached to the land, have always religiously worshiped it, always loved it as tenderly as a mother loves her child. They cherished the land even when it was not their own. They cultivated it, cared for it, and were proud and happy when the wheat stood high and the harvest was successful. An unfortunate drought filled their hearts with anxiety and distress, bitter tears fell from their dim eyes, and none was so unhappy as they. To the peasants there are no greater riches than the land. It is to them "finer than gold," it is the very source of their life, of their love, of

their happiness. We are reminded in almost every one of
their poems that nothing but the land was in the peasants'
minds when they came out to fight for the Revolution. It
would therefore be a mistake to think that they fought for
something else. Socialism, Collectivism, and Internationalism do not occupy a preeminent part in the peasants'
poetry. This is because they have never been imbued with
the Marxian doctrines, have never sympathized with them,
never surrendered to them. The same poet Essenin who
not long ago declared himself a Bolshevik says in his poem
"Home Again":

> No, I am not a communist . . . .
> . . . . The thick "Kapital"
> Or other books of Marx and Engels
> I have never read.

This is true of all the peasant poets, and Oreshin is cer-
tainly right when he affirms in his poem "The Great
Russian" that: "The International is not the Russian
Spirit."

It would be presuming too much to say that the peasants are hostile to the revolution. They responded to it
joyfully with many beautiful songs, yet one feels that they
do not sing the communistic state with all their hearts and
minds as do the proletarian poets. There are no sweeping
gestures in the peasant poetry, no empty phrases, no bitterness against their fellow-countrymen who belong to other
social classes. There is no desire for unceasing battle, destruction, and continuous civil war, but rather a wish to
forget all the horrors of the revolution.

A voice entreats us and teaches us
To think and comprehend.
We have not come into the world to destroy,
But to love and to trust.

                    —*Essenin.*

Our joy and our happiness
Are not noisy and clamorous.
They are more blissful and sweeter
Than a child's dreams . . . .

                    —*Kluyev.*

We have revolted more mightily than thunder
To see the sky sparkle like diamonds,
To grasp the praise of the angels,
To receive communion from the cup of our Saviour.

                    —*Idem.*

And the time must come soon, says Kluyev, when

The angels will pick forget-me-nots
From those meadows where lances were arrayed.

The appalling desolation which befell Russia in the
trying days of the blockade, of civil war, and of famine,
has not altered the peasants' faith in a brighter future,
and in the possibility of more friendly relations between
the various classes of Russia.

In the moment of sweet dreams,
Through the prism of grief, I see the time
When resuscitated friendship
Will make us all happy.

Man will calm down, and peacefully gaze
At everything alive.
To him the stir of wind will be a song,
And thunder—heavenly music.

Nature herself will weave a garment
From the warm, sunny rays,
Love and truth will breathe,
And life will flow like a stream.

—Kuzmichev.

The peasant scorns the ever antagonistic spirit of the city workingman. Being a devout Christian he is ready to forget the evils of the past, and to forgive those who caused them. Times have changed, therefore, the accumulated wisdom of the peasant tells him, there should be no antagonistic feeling, no more bitter enmity. The supreme needs of the country now are unity and common work, lest it fall a prey to the various factions and the foreign foes who are ready to tear it in pieces.

To change the ways
Of dark olden days,
We must work together
For our country dear.

.   .   .   .   .   .

Let disappear forever
The bitter enmity.
Let us unite together
For common work.

—Kuzmichev.

The outburst of exaltation over, the note of the peasant poetry becomes one of great and earnest warning. Beginning to feel more and more disgusted with the political excitements of the "red demons," who are interested in naught but the chances of a world revolution, the peasant poets solemnly warn them that in so acting they "will create new prisons for themselves'' (Oreshin). The peasants no longer want the subversive activities of the ''red demons'' (these two words are also Oreshin's), but moderation, wisdom, and justice.

We see, then, that the peasant poets showed a very sympathetic attitude toward the revolution. But having won the battle, having got full enjoyment of the land, they began to think how to use it properly. They advised the city workers to give up their visionary dreams of a world revolution and to occupy themselves with the important problems which beset Russia after November, 1917. Wishing now to make all the necessary efforts toward the realization of their potentialities, the peasants advocate in their poetry the idea of a united Russia bound together by the ties of blood, by the memory of its past sorrows, and by the purity of its spiritual aims.

CHAPTER III

THE RELIGIOUS ELEMENT IN PEASANT POETRY

Never will the Russian Peasant
Lose his faith in God . . . .
—*Oreshin.*

We are fellow brothers of Christ.
—*Kluyev.*

The November Revolution of 1917 has, for the first time in the history of Russia and of the world—save France, made an atheistic group of men the rulers of a great Empire. In trying to abolish all the old forms of life, these men came face to face with the greatest force of the past, religion. Now religion conflicts sharply with the cult of Marxism. Marxism may be fairly regarded as a new atheistic religion that strives to reduce to subjection not only the Orthodox church of Russia but all theistic beliefs. The attitude of its followers and prophets is essentially religious, not intellectual and open-minded. Basing its philosophy of life on purely materialistic principles, the Soviet government considered the deep religious attitude of the Russian peasantry especially harmful to its ideology. It therefore held the extirpation of formal religion to be one of its chief problems, and a clash at once arose between the two antagonistic forces, that of materialism and that of spirituality. The struggle of the Soviet government has been directed not against any particular confession of faith, but against all religious denominations, against all creeds. "Religion is opium to the people," ran the inscription on the official placards displayed on the walls of all public buildings, and also beside the sanctuaries most revered by the people. A definite warfare was declared against the church and the clergy. All the monasteries and church properties were nationalized and a great number of churches were closed. Some of these were reconstructed for the use of the Red army, and others were given over to various communistic organizations for the purpose of installing clubs, theatres, and motion pictures. To prove that religion was the last bulwark of the *bourgeoisie,* that it must become a nonentity, the atheistic government printed thousands of anti-religious pamphlets and books, and distributed them among the masses. Not only was the church separated from the state, but the government officials did all they could to encourage, deepen, and even openly to instigate church schisms. As a result of these activities the "Living Church" (*Zhivaya Tserkov*) came into being in May, 1922. The leaders of the "Living Church" try to adapt themselves to the Soviet rule. They condemn the national and international counter-revolution, and summon the citizens of Russia "to step forward in a united front and fight the world evil of social injustice together with the Soviet government." They brand all those who declared open war on the Bolsheviks, "monsters of the human race." But the orthodox do not take the

"Living Church" seriously. To them it is merely a communistic organization created for the sole purpose of destroying religion in all its manifestations. They have been opposed to it from the very beginning, and whenever they have to refer to it they call it the "False Church" (*Lzhivaya Tserkov*).

What strikes one most in reading contemporary popular poetry is the fact that in spite of the persecutions and the open propaganda of the Communists against the church, the peasants continue to proclaim their attachment to religion and their faith in God. Nothing as yet has been able to destroy the deeply religious attitude and the faithfulness to old traditions which have nourished the peasant soul for centuries.

> Imperishable in the Russian soul
> Are the psalms of our fathers and forefathers.
> —*Oreshin.*

In these words Oreshin expressed an undeniable truth regarding the nature of the peasant's soul and of his religious thought.

Hardly, however, could one apply Oreshin's words to all Russians. The cultured classes of Russian society had breathed in the prevailing currents of western European thought, had imbibed its philosophical and scientific systems, and had evolved a world of ideas which guided them in all their existence, including their spiritual experience. Contact with the thought of western Europe led them toward skepticism, and they naturally began to doubt and forget "the psalms of their fathers and their forefathers."

From time to time cultured Russians performed certain church duties, observed certain religious practices, but such habits were by no means a proof of spirituality, as understood by the peasants. With the urban workingmen, on the other hand, religious feeling has almost completely ceased to be. Scientific socialism and materialistic theories asserted their influence in all the avenues of the life and thought of this class of men, and they became more and more detached from "the psalms of their fathers and forefathers."

But it was not so with the "Russian soul," with the peasant. Abandoned as he always was, by force of circumstances, to his primitive and patriarchal mode of living, to his incoherent way of thinking, "the psalms of his fathers and forefathers" constituted his only spiritual nourishment. Through them he found a living inspiration in the deep silence of the vast steppes and in the whispering of the breeze among the leaves of the trees. Thanks to these psalms alone the peasant was enabled to perceive through the solemn gloom of the dense forests a heavenly light which brightened his dull life and gave a meaning to his hardships and his sufferings. Thus it has been in the past, and the peasant poetry gives us abundant evidence that it is still so in the present. The revolution, while lifting the weary and resigned peasant above his ordinary experiences, while dazzling him with new hopes, has not affected his old religious feelings. The psalms of his ancestors have remained even after the revolution: they are "imperishable." This is the reason why we find in almost every hymn to the revolution that spiritual tone and that deep-rooted religious element which have always made up the peasant's attitude toward life.

> From every side upon holy Russia
> New beliefs, new snares are thrown.
> But never will the Russian peasant
> Lose his faith in God.
> Neither wars, brought by tsars,
> Nor blood, nor executions, nor confusion,
> Will kill in the people's heart
> God's word and God's will.
>
> —*Oreshin.*

It is significant that the profound faith in "God's word" is still alive in the peasant's soul, is still being proclaimed aloud, even after the great revolutionary upheaval. And this faith of the peasant must be taken into account if Russia is ever to be understood. It explains why the peasants have found the Bolshevik religious persecutions so irksome, and why the Soviet government has had to become more tolerant in spiritual matters. The religious emotions of the peasants are too close to their hearts to be reached by any external attack. No woe, "no blood, nor executions" can erase from the peasant's soul "God's word and God's will." Through centuries of suffering and privation the Russian peasants have been supported by the faith that Christ is with those who suffer the most. From time immemorial they have repeated one of the oldest proverbs in the Russian language: "Whom God protects, none can harm." This has always served them as a reminder that in times of trouble they shall not fear any

earthly power, but shall have confidence in the supreme
strength of their protector. The peasants have never
wavered in the faith that the Almighty is just and merciful,
and they quite naturally rely on him alone. In the bitter
reality of their existence, in the harshness of their struggle
with nature and with their spiritual enemies, there shine
forever in the peasant's eyes ''God's word and God's will.''
Their notions of ''God's will'' may be vague, for ''unknown to men are God's ways,'' but the basic fact remains
that their faith in it is inextinguishable. It never fails
to arouse bright hopes in their tormented hearts, and to
illumine the arduous path of their life. ''God's word and
God's will'' remain for the peasants the greatest things in
all the world, the key to all mysteries, and the cure for all
their ills. In these troublous days when all Russia is
suffering the pangs of misery, the peasants raise their eyes
to heaven and sing:

> The healing cross
> Is our guide and will . . . .
> —*Kluyev.*

''The healing cross'' also gives them strength to bear their
sufferings silently, it teaches them to accept the cruel
afflictions of life serenely, for the fatalistic Russian pro-
verb: ''From fate one cannot escape,'' is still deeply
engraved on their hearts.

The Russian peasants are faithful believers and not
speculative seekers after God, as are many of their intellectual brethren. They do not question the existence of
God. It is clear and obvious to them that God exists.

Were it otherwise, there would be no reason for the existence of the world. This basic fact is with the peasants an
unquestioning faith which has been absolutely blended with
their mental attitude toward life.

> We are blessed, always faithful,
> We believe, we love, we are calm.
> The secret of God and of the universe
> We keep deep in our bosom.
>
> *—Kluyev.*

What simple and stern faith, and how different from that
of the Russian intellectuals! The vision of God and the
universe which the great majority of cultured Russians
hold is much more complex than that of the peasants; the
intellectuals have never possessed the peaceful and calm
serenity of the common folk. And one wonders whether
Tolstoy and other Russian novelists, poets, and philosophers
have not been right in pointing to the "simple people" as
the real "apostles of Christianity." The great difference
between the faith of the peasants and that of the intellectuals becomes clearer when one turns to the heroes of
Tolstoy, to Pierre Bezukhov and Levin, for instance. It
will be remembered that when these cultured men aspire
to God, their craving is always for that faith which lives
forever in the credulous soul of the humble peasant. And
it is always that "secret of God" which the peasant keeps
deep in his bosom that resuscitates the hearts of the intellectuals.

Vain seems the hope that by making a confession of
the absolute emptiness of one's life in this civilized world

of ours, the gleam of true faith will penetrate into one's soul. To believe so strongly and so naturally as the Russian peasants do, one must draw from the very roots, from the very fount of their life, from their simple imaginative presentation of the universe, and from their unquestionable acceptance of the existence of God. To be "always faithful, blessed, and calm" requires an elemental strength that most Russian intellectuals do not possess. Only to the "always faithful" does prayer offer a real and beneficent solace in this world. It is the peasant who in our days of topsy-turvydom still finds time to pause in front of the shrines and murmur a prayer to Christ.

> We are still faithfully praying to Christ.
> —*Essenin.*

> Kiss the blessed earth as you would kiss
> A cross in a church.
> Pray for the natural riches of Russia
> And remember, while praying,
> That Christ still watches
> From out the dense clouds,
> From the high blue hills.
> —*Oreshin.*

The same Christ who still seems to watch the peasant "from the high blue hills" also continues to watch him with mysterious eyes from the time-blackened ikon hanging in the corner of his hut. The peasant still kneels before the ikon, still pays homage to it, and still offers tapers to the Saviour or the Saint within its frame.

> I made an oath before the ikon
> To become peaceful and holy.
> —*Kluyev.*

> To the peasant's Saviour offer a taper;
> Goodness and love are incarnate in him.
>
>   *—Oreshin.*
>
> I am praying before thee,
> O broken ikon! . . . .
>
>   *—Fomin.*

The tinge of the mystical about the ikon still holds the imagination of the Russian peasantry.[1]

With most of the peasant poets Christ is not an inaccessible deity living somewhere afar in lofty regions, but an ever present force. Christ is on earth, among the peasants; he seldom leaves them, and they see him everywhere.

> Through the village with a knapsack Christ was walking
> In white, silvery garments.
> Powerfully and loudly Christ was singing
> Of the inconsolable peasant's sorrow.
>
>   *—Oreshin.*
>
> I see Christ in the church, on the road,
> In the guise of a beggar, in rags and dust. . . . .
>
>   *—Kluyev.*
>
> Through the pines, through the firs,
> Through the waving birches,
> With the crown of thorns,
> I perceive Christ Jesus.
>
>   *—Essenin.*

In their simplicity of heart the peasants regard Christ as a tiller of the soil tending the crops.

---

[1] The fact that the peasants do not want to part with the ikons seems to be the despair of Trotsky, who hopelessly states in his *Problems of Life* (pp. 40, 41): "Ikons still hang in the home. . . . . The bulk of the people are not affected by anti-religious propaganda."

> Christ, bending, is tilling the soil.
> —*Malashkin.*

> Christ is watching over the fields.
> —*Borissov.*

This constant communion with Christ renders the peasants'
religious experience more vivid, more personal. It sancti-
fies their humble life and is a signal to them to endure their
sufferings and calamities with fortitude.

The Saints, too, dwell among the peasants. They walk
along the roads, through the villages and the fields, and
share all the earthly pain, all the miseries and sorrows that
fall to the lot of the peasants.

> Our little father Nicholas
> In a coarse gray coat
> Is walking through the fields . . . .
> Each morning with bitter tears
> He weeps over Russia. . . . .
> —*Oreshin.*

> Like a pilgrim Saint Nicholas
> Is walking along the road.
> He communes with God
> And brings help to the needy peasants.
> —*Kluyev.*

The "little father Nicholas" is with those who "were born
in chains and who will die free" (Oreshin). Together
with the revolted peasants, who are now "free as Stenka
Razin[2] and holy as Christ," Saint Nicholas takes a practical part in their fight for land and a brighter future.

---

[2] A Volga brigand of the seventeenth century.

> Through the fields walks
> Upright Saint Nicholas,
> The image vestments, like the redness of dawn,
> Are seen in the villages.
> The Saint is strolling through the fields
> Gathering his fellow-soldiers.
> Come out into the open fields,
> O Russia of mine, my beloved!
> The executioner's block and noose
> Have disappeared from the fields forever.
> Glory to those who fell for freedom,
> For holy freedom.
>   —*Oreshin.*

And when the poet, always intent as he is upon the land problem, asks:

> To whom, dear Nicholas, should belong
> The land, the fields, and the villages?

the upright saint answers:

> To you my brothers and sons, to you alone.

Not all the peasant poets, however, picture Saint Nicholas as a fighter for land and freedom. To Essenin, for instance, the saint appears rather as a poet and contemplator, a Russian Francis d'Assisi, enamored of the beauty of God's world.

> In a hat of cloud-like form
> Shod with bast, himself like a phantom,
> Mikola the pilgrim moves about
> Through many a village and town.
>
> On his shoulders he carries a knapsack,
> A holy banner and two strings,
> He walks and softly sings
> The psalms from Jordan.

The evil sorrow and the evil grievance
Vanished into the cold distance.
And the blue heaven's domes
Are kindled like scarlet dawns.

Bowing low their gentle faces,
A row of weeping willows dreamt,
And like silken rosaries
Their pearly branches bent.

Walks the kind, saintly man,
Down his cheeks runs the sweat, like holy oil:
— O my forest, my merry dancer,
Lull to sleep thy weary stranger.
All living creatures the pilgrim calls
And feeds them millet from his stole.

                                   —*Essenin.*

Saint Nicholas, as pictured by Essenin, is "an inhabitant of another world." He is walking peacefully toward "God's temple" where the "gentle Saviour," in "purple vestments," is awaiting him. And the poet, meeting the saint, implores him "to pray to the Saviour for the poor peasants." The saint of Oreshin, on the contrary, is an inhabitant of this world, living with the peasants in their untidy huts, bearing deep in his heart their sufferings, and participating in their fight for land and freedom. With Essenin the earth is enamored of heaven, with Oreshin, in his own words, "heaven is enamored of earth."

Every peasant poet pictures Christ and the saints from his own angle of vision, but all express the same austere faith that has its roots in the vigorous, fruitful Russian soil. All peasant poets show a strong attachment to tradition, and most of their poems bear the unmistakable stamp

of the religious songs, legends, and folk-tales of the past.
As in the days of long ago the Holy Virgin still protects
the peasants and prays for them.

> Christ is sitting in white attire,
> And the Holy Virgin, on her knees,
> For the peasants is praying with bitter tears.
>
> *—Tsarev.*

Though encumbered with novel fancies and fads, the contemporary peasant poetry still reflects the soul of old
Russia. As of old the peasants still sanctify everything
around them, and the sacred images of days gone by still
appeal irresistibly to their imagination.

> The peasants' huts are like garbed images . . . .
> The fields are like holy legends.
> The groves have an ikon's nimbus.
> The rosaries are ringing melody
> On willows, the humble sisters.
>
> *—Essenin.*

> In a humble ikon in the chapel wise old Mikola,
> With a dimmed visage, thinks peasants' thoughts.
>
> *—Oreshin.*

> Anon the dove from Jordan
> Soars high above the land,
> In the bast cradle of a peasant
> Is fast asleep Salvation's infant. . . . .
> The peasant's feast is holy and serene
> In the Saviour's fertile Eden.
> In the fir tree the bird Sirin[3]
> Will sing the lullaby again.
>
> *—Kluyev.*

---

[3] "Sirin" is the name for screech owl.

The prevalence of the religious tone of this imagery gives to the peasant poems the fragrance of church incense. From the examples quoted above it is easy to see how mysticism still surrounds the Russian peasantry of today. The church to which they belong from birth has not yet rejected that mysticism. Neither has it cast away the spirit and the ideal of Christian faith, and the peasantry still cling to these, in spite of the religious persecutions of the Soviet government.

"We are fellow-brothers of Christ"—says the peasant poet Kluyev, and this shows clearly that the pervading love of God still survives in the peasant's soul. But to be "fellow-brothers of Christ" one must be able to forgive, as He did. And indeed we have seen in the preceding chapter that the peasants are ready to forgive and forget all the evil done to them in the past. Passages to this effect abound in their poetry.

> O Russia mine, torn in pieces! . . . .
> I am prostrate before thy wounds.
> Forgive, O mother mine,
> Let us forget the horrors of the past.
> —*Fomin.*

Such is the lofty and charitable spirit of the "fellow brothers of Christ." The peasants know that only through Christian love can Russia, now "torn in pieces," be regenerated. Their poetry testifies that the belief in Christian love which rises clearly above all contradictions, is strong within them.

It is important to notice that the peasant poets, in their clinging to the divine, in their longing for the unknown, and in their desire to perceive the beyond, are akin to the Russian symbolists, whether philosophers or poets, particularly to V. Soloviev (1853–1900), A. Bely (1880–) and A. Blok (1880–1921). Like the symbolists, the peasant poets, also, are tormented by

> That which has no name,
> Which, like a hint, by its mystery torments.
> —*Kluyev.*

This mystical state of mind is the wish of the soul to sink into and merge with God and interpret the reality of the world from within. It is essentially a desire to comprehend the relation of God, truth, wisdom, and beauty, and to grasp inwardly the spiritual laws of the universe. Like the peasant poets, the Russian symbolists have made materialism their main ground of attack. They also await the revelation of Saint Sophia, the wisdom of God in his purpose to redeem humanity.

> I await in silence Thy withheld and worshiped grace,
> I await to know, I await an answer. . . . .
> —*Blok.*

In their desire to grasp the Infinite and the intangible Beyond, the peasant poets gaze at the sky and seem to hear the heavenly music of the angels.

> He who is alive, whose soul is not hardened,
> Sees the skies and hears the heavenly music.
> —*Essenin.*

In the enchantment of this mood and in this frame of mind the peasant poets, like the symbolists, aspire to another, to a better and ideal world.

I long for the heavenly secrets
For the shores of another world. . . . .
                                    —*Kluyev.*

This same idea was expressed by Soloviev when he said:

. . . . I walked where dawn-lit mists were lying
To find the shores of wonder and mystery.

We see thus that while the peasant expected from the
revolution land and freedom for his earthly comfort, he
nevertheless did not forget to seek heaven as the final
resting place. The peasant's individualism indeed is not
solely due to the economic factors of his life, the owning
and tilling of the soil individually, but is also the result
of his spiritual conception of the universe and of God,
whose secret he keeps in his bosom. This conception must
make the peasant an individualist. For one can know God,
or apprehend the laws of the Infinite, only through the
inner disposition of the soul.

The potent voice of contemporary peasant poetry is
religion. The faith in the beneficence of the Holy Spirit,
in the divinity of the Saviour, in the eternity of the soul,
and in existence beyond the grave, is not an outward mode
of expression with the peasant poets, but the very state of
their mind and heart. This faith permeates and animates
all their poems. And this is no matter for surprise, for,
as we have seen, this faith is the principal melody in the
symphony of their life. It therefore vibrates in their
poetry with the emotion and ecstasy of true religious
experience.

CHAPTER IV

LOVE OF RUSSIA IN PEASANT POETRY

My Russia! . . . .
Awful and beauteous thou art!
            —*A. Homyakov.*

O native country, how beauteous thou art!
                        —*Oreshin.*

Sometimes Russia weeps apart,
And all those tears, unseen, unmeasured,
Our poetry has caught and treasured.
                    —*N. Minsky.*

O Russia! . . . I love thy silent grief.
                    —*Essenin.*

Love of mother country is, of course, no new theme in
Russian poetry. Poignantly expressed by the anonymous
bard of the *Tale of Igor's Host,* the first national epic
(about 1200), this theme has, in subsequent years, adorned
the works of all Russian poets. There is no doubt, in the
Russian mind at least, that since the first Tartar invasion
the feeling of love for the native land has grown ring by
ring like a tree, with its roots deep in a vigorous and fertile
soil, nourished by the unyielding perseverance of centuries.
Little wonder, then, that in contemporary peasant poetry
love of mother country is, after religion, the most distin-
guishing element. All the peasant poets, indeed, as if they
had by poetic expression communicated with their prede-

cessors, are filled with enthusiasm for their native country, and continue to express their admiration and love for it in the same strain sung by all the prerevolutionary poets.

In marked contrast to the peasant poets are their proletarian contemporaries, to whom the subject of love of country seems unsuitable and unsavory. Here again we must notice the discord of the voices of these two social classes, the one deeply national, the other broadly international. Rising in stark opposition to the very notion of mother country, the proletarian poets widen more and more the gulf between their psychology and that of the peasants. Clinging to their visionary doctrines, the followers of Lenin and Trotsky employ their fiery energy of mind in the creation and propagation of broad internationalism. With them even the word "Russia" has gone out of fashion, and has made way for the letters "U. S. S. R." (Union of Socialist Soviet Republics). Aiming at distant horizons they forget even the name of their own country. Moreover, they always deride the intensely nationalistic and patriotic feelings of the peasant poets as shallow delusions. The very existence of such feelings seems to the proletarian poets to stultify, in some degree at least, the cause for which the disciples of the "Dictatorship of the Proletariat" have fought. They therefore never hesitate to give vent to the most distasteful views about patriotism. In this term they see nothing but the spirit of conquest and of military dominion against which almost the whole world was striving in the last war. Patriotism and imperialism are thus to the proletarian poets one and the same thing. And because their teachers, the Russian Social Democrats, have in the past interpreted the word imperialism as a hideous repression of freedom, the proletarian poets assume now that the Russian empire —for the peasants still call it an empire—must mean the same hateful thing. As for traditions, they simply abhor them, because in things of the past they see a great hindrance to the advancement and the strengthening of the proletarian cause. Being adepts of pure materialism, they extol city life, rejoice in it, and lend a deaf ear to mother nature.

At quite the opposite pole stand the peasant poets, who are not so easily influenced by mere words. They do not talk so much of humanity, but neither do they forget man; they do not aim at an international paradise, and they never forget their own country. They are nationalists to the core, and they have never lacked patriotism. ''Our souls are God's, our bodies the Tsar's''—the peasants used to say in prerevolutionary days. The Tsar is no more, but the peasants continue to love their mother country deeply and reverently. They still live in the old traditions, in the ancient popular sayings and songs, for

> How can one forget the ancient sayings,
> The gray distance of the past,
> The great sufferings of our fathers,
> Their needs and sorrows mirrored in their songs?
>
> —*Yaropolov.*

The peasant poets still draw their inspiration from the treasures of folklore, and the harmony of the past is thus preserved in their poetry of the present. They adorn their language with the symbols of old Russia, and symbolize everything around them, even the humblest activities of their life. They have a wonderful gift of dreaming. They often muse and behold the beauties of the infinite spaces of the steppes. In the fields they see the mirror of an omnipotent power, a reflection of "many-colored wisdom and beneficence." The dark blue sky and the shining stars in heaven, trembling in silence, convey to them a reverent feeling of awe. The restless, busy, noisy city is not to their taste; they adore the life of the village where they can revel in colors. They love to hear the rustling of the grass and the murmur of the mighty forest and the little brook. Mother nature draws the peasant poets like a magnet, and they feel her secrets with a throbbing heart.

With tenderness of feeling and with deep emotion do the peasant poets sing their love of Russia.

> O my beautiful Rus, thou hast
> The spirit and might of a giant. . . . .
> Under thy gray dowlas shirt
> A turbulent force abides.
>
> I behold thee downtrodden,
> But in thee I honor ever
> Thy passion, thy latent vigor,
> And thy dream's fiery ardor. . . . .
> —*Morozov.*
>
> O Rus, the raspberry plain,
> The azure sunk in the stream.
> I love with ecstasy and pain
> Thy sorrow, like the lake, crystalline . . . .
> —*Essenin.*

O native country, how beauteous thou art!
How adorable are
Thy rye steppes, thy rye people,
Thy rye sun. Even thy songs
Smell of soil and rye.
                              —*Oreshin.*

    Thy life and thy wounds,
    Thy gloomy plains,
    I will not change
    For any country in the world.

    I breathe in thy sorrow
    And in thy bitter mead.
    Before thy salted rye crumb
    I prostrate myself in rapture.

    And repeating tenderly
    In verses: ''Peasant'' and ''Russia''
    For my dear mother country
    I weep and laugh.

             —*Druzhinin.*

I love thee, native land,
I adore thy gloomy face,
Thy fields, thy pine groves,
And the dense forests in the summer heat.

Beloved country! All that is thine
Is close and dear to me.
The forgotten tombs of the fathers,
The deep silence of the cemeteries. . . . .

And I, thy son, pursued by fate,
Am always anxious and grieved,
For thee alone, country beloved,
All my life I pray.
                              —*Yaropolov.*

The knapsack on my shoulders will remain,
Alone I will wander among men.
Mother country, even the wandering son loves thee,
Receive me, dear mother, take me to thyself.

Beyond the Carpathians, in Hungary and in Poland
I wandered, but there I felt distressed.
My grief I could bear no longer,
To thy fields I returned, O mother.

Is it my fault that the call
Of my mother country clutched my soul?
I will not disturb thy peace,
In my songs to thee I find my ease.
                                        —*Artamonov.*

The Russia that all the peasant poets sing with such
depth of feeling is the peasants' Russia. To them these
two words, "peasant" and "Russia," are synonymous, two
symbols with the same meaning: the dear mother country.
They love her "unto joy and pain," and even her sorrows
and wounds are dear to them. In the vastness of the "rye
steppes" and in the "raspberry plains" they see something
wonderful and awe-inspiring, something which grips their
hearts, and which forces upon them the realization of an
enormous, "giant-like strength." When away from their
mother country, they feel like children stranded and lost,
and it is to her that they return and bring their sorrows
and joys, their admiration and love. Full of bright hopes,
for under their mother's "gray dowlas shirt" they perceive a great living force, they pray for Russia with passionate devotion, and always whisper to her gentle and
caressing words.

> I love my poor Russia,
> And for her I pray. . . . .
> —*Dudorov.*

My mother country, how thoughtful and tender thou art!
> —*Essenin.*

> Be patient, my poor, suffering
> Mother country, forgotten by fortune . . . .
> Soon we too shall be happy
> And the bright sun will shine over thee. —*Golikov.*

> Shattered ikon,—
> Lacerated Russia mine!
> My heart is broken,
> I pray for thee. —*Fomin.*

Russia, a "shattered ikon," becomes the symbol of sanctity, and in their imagination the peasant poets see her under the light of a holy flame.

> The hut is a chariot, the corners are the wheels,
> The seraphs will alight from the cloudy spheres.
> Peasant Russia, in a great procession,
> Will float aloft to meet the challenging storms.
> —*Kluyev.*

The love of mother country is fuel to the fire of poetic imagination in the peasant bards. To some of them Russia appears in the image of a "rye sun," to others in the image of a triumphant "chariot." And the angels descending from heaven seem to inspire in peasant Russia a longing to "float aloft" and courageously meet the "challenging storms." Russia with her huts and green-domed churches is to the peasant poets a God-given cradle. And at all times, in all conditions, they listen intently to the sad lullaby of their adored mistress.

> O dear country, beloved weariness!
> I recognize thy lullaby even without words,
> Living cradle of mine!
> —*Druzhinin.*

The tone of this sad lullaby is invariably the same throughout all Russia. From the gray north, with its roaring wind, snow, and cold, to the smiling south, with its sunlit golden days, this song passes like the murmur of a mournful lament, and carries with it an inexpressible sadness. Deep into the bosom of the Russian the profound melancholy of this song has penetrated and has wrapped his soul in a keen and poignant pain.

Under the despotism of Nicholas I, Gogol had written:

"Russia! Russia! . . . . Why does the mournful song that floats over all the length and breadth of thee from sea to sea echo unceasingly in the ear? What is in it, in that song? What is it that calls and sobs and clutches at my heart? What are these strains that so poignantly greet me, that go straight to my soul, that throb about my heart?"

And the peasant poets seem to try to answer Gogol's question:

> Sad song, thou art the pain of Russia. . . . .
> Happy he who could interpret
> Thy pastoral sadness as joy,
> O beloved Russia mine!
> —*Essenin.*

> There is a vast country upon the earth,
> There grow the pine trees and the firs;
> It is desolate, and it is unknown,
> And it is the cradle of Russia's woe.
> —*Kluyev.*

This melancholy tone of the peasant poets must not be interpreted as a sign of protest against the sad external

surroundings of their life. It is rather an inner chord of
their soul, grave and prayerful. Sorrow to a Russian
is not a calamity. He seldom tries to avoid it, and fatal-
istically accepts it, almost as a blessing.

> I love the rumble of stormy seas,
> And the glitter of stars on the waves.
> The blessed suffering,
> And the blessing people.
> I love the rumble of stormy seas.
>
> —*Essenin.*

Almost every Russian treasures his sorrow and, like some
of the heroes of Dostoyevsky, believes that through it he
may perceive the truth. Hence his invincible faith in
the blessedness of sorrow, his extraordinary patience and
endurance in life.

> I deeply treasure my sorrow,
> And my singing heart is calm,
> O how I do long for my sorrow,
> Not knowing who and where she is. . . . .
>
> —*Klychkov.*

The Russian paintings and musical compositions of
which the subjects are taken from the life of the mother
country reveal the same sorrowful tone that we find in
peasant poetry. When one looks on Russian landscapes or
listens to her "Pathetic Symphonies," an indescribable
emotion grips one's soul and penetrates into its very
depths. The Russian landscape may, at first sight, seem
monotonous: a narrow, endless road, or a wide, flat, barren
plain, a snow-hidden peasant hut, a tiny, forlorn-looking
domed church, a lonely village cemetery, a small wooden

fence, and a windmill in the far distance. But all this conveys a deep and unforgetable impression, as if mother nature had scattered through Russia a grave and magical charm. The Russian landscape weighs heavily upon one's heart, but it nevertheless remains for a long time in the memory as a recollection haunting alike in its tone, its beauty, its silence, and its mystery. Peasant Russia, with her tales, her epics, her traditions, and her ancient songs has always been an inspiration to the Russian composers. The peasant poet Shiriayev is right when he says:

> We have nourished with songs, with our bright tales
> Not only the Pushkins, but also the Korsakovs. . . . .

All the Russian folk melodies express a wide and varied range of emotion. Like the landscapes, the music often speaks of great monotony, of solitude, and of the mother country's sorrow. No matter what Russian melody one hears, one feels running through it the deep, age-long emotions of the people. And the peasant poets who draw their inspiration from the past of their native land will certainly serve as a link with the Russia of the future. The grief of the mother country, as expressed in her paintings, her music, and her poetry, is boundless, but not to love her, not to trust in her, is for the peasant poets, as well as for the Russian intellectuals, absolutely impossible.

> One cannot fathom thy cold grief;
> On a misty shore thou art,
> But not to love thee, not to trust thee—
> This I cannot do, I cannot master.
>
> *—Essenin.*

These verses of Essenin call to memory the words of the
Slavophil poet Tyutchev (1803–1873), who said of Russia
in the days of tsardom:

> Russia cannot by mind be known,
> There is no common measure holds her,
> She has a stature of her own,
> He who believes in her beholds her.[1]

After reading these passages from their poetry we know
that the peasant poets trust in Russia unreservedly, just as
did Tyutchev, Fet (1820–1892), Homyakov (1804–1860),
and all those national poets who felt deeply the spirit and
the soul of their mother country and of her people.

It has been noticed in the preceding chapter that the
peasant poets are very much akin to the Russian symbolists.
This is particularly noticeable in poems where the subject
of mother country is touched upon. To the symbolists
Russia has always been a sacred thing, a fount of love and
inspiration.

> Oh Russia, beloved mine! Unto pain
> We feel thy long road. . . . .
> Ours is the steppe road, the road of endless sorrow,
> But of thy sorrow, O Russia,
> Even of thy long night's gloom,
> I am not afraid. . . . .
> Such as my Russia is,
> She is dearer to me than any other country.
> —*A. Blok.*

And we have seen that the peasant poets too ''will not
change Russia for any other country in the world.''

---

[1] Translated by Sir Bernard Pares.

> Mother Russia, to thee are my songs,
> O dumb, stern mother.
> I know everything. . . . . Perhaps I do not know?
> But I love, love, love thee.
> > > *—A. Bely.*

The peasant poets sing their songs to Russia, for she is dearer to them than paradise.

> If the heavenly host should decree:
> Forsake thy Rus and live in Eden—
> No paradise for me—I will say then:
> Give back my country to me!
> > > *—Essenin.*

Like the peasants, the symbolists were enamored of Russia's glory, and showed great pride in her elemental strength.

> Halt here, as Oedipus once halted
> Before the sphinx's enigmatic eyes.
> > > *—A. Blok.*

The symbolist and the peasant poets regard Russia as the greatest and strongest of all countries, and it is from her that they all await a message to the world. Russia is the Messiah who will bring a precious gift to all.

> Thou, elemental force,—
> Russia, Russia, Russia,—
> Art the Messiah of the coming days.
> > > *—A. Bely.*
> I have touched thy wounds,
> Of a sudden thy secrets I fathom.
> Thou art a fairy tale, a legendary song
> In the glitter of everlasting stars.
> > > *—Fomin.*

Russia's noble traditions and the bright hopes of the symbolists and other prerevolutionary poets are not dead in contemporary peasant poetry. Deeply loving their mother country, the peasant poets prostrate themselves before her wounds, and pray for her alone, because it is the fate of their native land that torments their hearts. The sufferings of the mother country purify the souls of the peasant poets, and rouse their muse to fresh creations. Jealously and reverently guarding and valuing the rust and the gold of the past, listening attentively to the voices of their ancestors, the peasant poets are recreating the poem of the "shattered ikon," of their beloved mother country, of their Holy Russia.

CHAPTER V

LOVE OF NATURE IN PEASANT POETRY

My friends are the fields, the forests,
The dawn of spring, the storm's thunder . . . .
                                        —*Essenin.*
Mother—Nature, I am all thine . . . .
                                        —*Fomin.*
I sing that there's much joy in life,
Such an intoxicating wilderness in the green fields . . . .
                                        —*Radimov.*
To kiss thee, my earth, I come . . . .
                                        —*Druzhinin.*

The peasant poets reveal to us not only their joyful enthusiasm for the revolution, their religious instinct, their attachment to old traditions, and their veneration for their native land, but also their love of nature. It would be impossible to get a clear understanding of the spirit of peasant poetry without considering all the elements it contains. And love of nature is a very significant element in that poetry. The peasant's emotional attitude toward nature gives us a better insight into his whole mode of thought.

Mother Nature awakens in the peasant poets a gracious mood; to her their hearts make a ready response; she is a friend to whom they can safely confide all their secrets. Between Mother Nature and the soul of the peasant there is always a sympathetic intelligence. They are hers, and as they look at her work, they seem to understand her mysteries and all her processes and laws. That is why she inspires them with the deepest affection and love.

> I know the murmur of the ringing
> Corn that ripens in its sleep,
> The fragrant rye's greetings
> To my native country.
>
> I love the aftermath of green,
> The rows of sickles and the blade's sheen,
> The rustling whirl of the vagabond wind
> Amidst the silvery birch trees.
> —*Oreshin.*

Every line of their poems breathes the air of the vast, infinite space. Be the sky smiling or overcast with clouds, be it stark winter or glorious spring, their love for nature is always profound, humble, reverent, sacred.

> The wilderness of native plain,
> The vernal murmur of the groves,
> And the cries of the cranes
> To me are dearer than any fame. . . . .
> —*Klychkov.*
>
> Disheveled and tousled—I am a peasant
> Smelling of the green mint.
> For thee—my virgin land
> All the live-long day I long.
>
> Thee—my fallow field,
> My joy, my sweat and blood,
> All my life long did I bemoan
> Standing at the gates in times of flood.

> In the bloody fight I pine;
> Into the fields, tender and meek, I go,
> And with a prayer, as of old,
> To kiss thee, my earth, I come. . . . .   —*Druzhinin.*

Mother Nature has drawn the peasant poets close to her bosom. Even when her moods are most severe, they always feel in her touch a friendly hand that chases away the sorrow from their brows, and lifts the pain from their oppressed hearts. The "disheveled and tousled" peasant hears the powerful and mighty call of the earth, and "the fields" become his "joy," his "sweat," and his "blood." In a prayerful mood, "tender and meek," he goes to plough and to scatter the grain, and the "murmur of the ringing corn" is to him a soft melody of infinite sweetness. The peasant's longing for the "virgin land" is strong indeed, for he lives and thinks "with every grass blade, with every ear of wheat," and all his being becomes a part of them.

> The native fields are my body,
> And there, upon the roads, is my soul . . . .
> —*Fomin.*

So the fields do not appear to the peasant simply as an image of an immence ocean, nor are the tall stalks of wheat trembling in the breeze, merely glittering waves; they are to him something more: his very existence, his soul, his body. No wonder that he loves "the aftermath of green," the "silvery birch trees," the "wilderness of the native plain," the cries of cranes, and the golden straw on the roofs of Russian hamlets. All these are dearer to him "than any fame." And he kisses the earth as the symbol of life and inspiration.

Not all men behold nature in the same light. The aspect in which Mother Nature appears to one who is gazing upon her depends largely on his state of mind and his mood. The city dwellers are usually not so receptive and sensitive to nature's call as are the peasants, who see in all her manifestations the expression of the divine. And, unlike the city dwellers, they regard the meadows, fields, and forests as their nearest fellow-beings, as god-given friends. They nestle on the bosom of Mother Nature, and receive from her body nourishment for their soul and imagination. They therefore feel with great intensity the pulsating heart of nature herself, and perceive her "wonderful mystery."

> Whenever I gaze upon the field, upon the skies,
> In the field and in the heavens there is paradise. . . . .
> *—Essenin.*

> There's no more wonderful mystery,
> There's no other beauty,
> Than to scatter the grains of song
> O'er the virgin soil in spring!
> O my forest, meadow, field!
> Let it be so all my life! . . . .   *—Klychkov.*

> There is nothing more prayerful, beautiful,
> Than the hermit-huts in the ocean of rye,
> When beyond the heated fields of purple
> The incense is burned by the pines . . . . *—Fomin.*

In the dawns of spring, when the earth frees herself from the bondage of ice, and life, under the reviving rays of the sun, is astir anew, the peasant feels deeply the throbbing of the soil which he is tilling. It is then that he views the workings of nature with serene joy, and learns to appreciate the symbolic value of "Mother Earth."

There is the Mother Earth, the Life's Fount,
Amidst the rich, deep, and poor lands.
Her guardian is Fate, and her gardener is God.
To her, through life's dusk, there leads no road.

Only her daughter—Fallow Land—in the harrowing season
Reveals, like a scroll, Destiny's decrees;
The tiller reads them, and so does Someone else with him:
'Tis he who rules o'er the fire and the soul of the peasant.
                                        —*Kluyev.*

The peasant poets, being simple, natural, elemental,
earnestly listen to the never-ending murmur of "Mother
Nature," and "Mother Earth" is to them "Life's Fount."
In their direct and close contact with nature, they see her
grow radiantly alive in the spring, and wither in the fall
when "the fogs spread like a mournful pall over the green
fields." Because of their constant communion with Mother
Nature, and their primitive way of living, the peasant
poets, beholding forever the same horizon, merge themselves
entirely with her. That is why "Fallow Land" reveals to
them, "like a scroll, Destiny's decrees," which only the
tiller and the God above him can read. They ardently
love "Mother Earth" not only for the future harvest she
will bring them as a reward for their hard toil, but also
for the creative forces, for the hopes and joys she arouses
in their souls.

It is not only the time "when all the sky is aflame with
dawn" that the peasant poets glorify in their songs of
praise; every season of the year possesses for them its own
charm, and yields them a keen joy.

What a sorrow all around! The fogs spread
Like a mournful pall o'er the green fields,

And windy blasts, scattering the autumn leaves
Tear from the boughs the purple and brocade.
How sad it is! Beyond the hillock a song weeps,
And the poplar alley moans of the past,
Crying, upon the wide heavens the cranes float,
And beyond the river grief rises like gray mist.

—Radimov.

The autumn, cold, meek, and kind,
Steals into the russet yard at twilight;
And through the blue window panes
A golden-haired lad gazes upon the jackdaws' game.

—Essenin.

All is drowsy in the river, all is quiet on the plain;
Only burdock and wormwood grow upon the mound.
In the skies there floats a cloudy chain.
A lonely star glitters above the mound.

It is time for prayer: come out and say prayers,
Bow to the bright plain, the star, the wind,
And to our father: he is buried in the mound 'midst the fields,
Now make your sacrifice for his eternal peace.

All is drowsy in the river. The were-wolf guards the ways.
The peasant stands lonely by night at his prayer:
To the field, the wind, the star he prays . . . .
Into eternity the hazy distance flees away.

—Radimov.

How pathetic is this autumn song and how sad is the sight when "the windy blasts, scattering the autumn leaves, tear from the boughs the purple and brocade." How desolate are the poplar's "moans of the past," of the time when all nature was alive and radiated light and joy. And yet, in spite of the somber picture all around, the peasant stands lonely in the gray fog and prays "to the field, the wind, and the star."

After the dark and sorrowful autumn the peasant poets reveal to us the magnetic charm and beauty of winter.

> Across the first snow I ramble,
> In my heart—the white lily of the awakening might,
> O'er my path the star is lighted at night
> Like a blue candle.
>
> . . . .
>
> O white plain, thou art full of beauty!
> My blood tingles with light frost!
> I long to press to my body
> The birches' naked breasts.
>
> O, the woody and dense darkness!
> O, the joy of snow-clad fields!
> My arms are hungry for an embrace
> Of the willows' wooden thighs.
>
> —*Essenin.*

The white plains of "the first snow" are truly "full of beauty." The branches of the trees are adorned with laces of fanciful designs that cannot be imitated by human hands. And everything around, from the blue sky to the fields, has an air of infinite charm. It is not so much the bitter frost that makes the peasant's blood tingle when he gazes upon the "snow-clad fields"; it is rather that overwhelming rapture, which fills him with a desire to "embrace the willow's thighs," and to feel thus in that contact the tender love of Mother Nature.

The peasant poets abandon themselves to the music of the woods, fields and rivers. Mother Nature has a wonderful magnetism for their souls. And it is her praise that they always softly sing; to her they bring their humble and quiet prayers, for she is to them the most precious treasure.

> I sing always, a born singer I am,
> My verse I write not with ink;
> I wander in the woods in the early morn,
> And tend my sheep by the stream.

> I sing fairy-tales
> 'Mid the murmur of splashing water . . . .
> I am a shepherd,
> And my abode is—the soft, green plains. . . . .
>   —*Fomin.*
> To the scarlet dawns I pray,
> And I partake of the holy sacrament by the river.
>   —*Essenin.*
> My father whets his scythe near the barn,
> Beyond the woods there blows the horn . . . .
> I long for no other Eden
> Than this peaceful corner of Earth. . . . .
>   —*Fomin.*

The magic power of nature strikes in the peasant's heart a vibrating, musical chord, and her murmur and sweet melodies reverberate in his simple soul. Ardently does he sing nature's wild beauty, her charm, her brilliance, her gravity, and her sadness, for he is "a born singer." The pale glamor of dawn, the first rays of the sun piercing the dense mist, the deep red flush of the evening glow, a nightly vigil on some moonlit hill, under the sparkling stars above—all this creates in the peasant poet's mind a host of indelible impressions. The whisper of the birch and fir trees that he hears while wandering in the woods or guarding his sheep, all nature's sounds floating in the air, arouse in him deep emotions, and his soul radiates gladness, joy, and happiness. In such a bright mood, while gazing at the "soft, green plans" and flowery meadows; while listening to the rippling trill of the "splashing water" in which the sunbeams mirror themselves and sparkle like diamonds, the peasant poets sing their "fairy tales." And the horn's call that they hear "from beyond the wood" on a calm summer afternoon does not arouse in their souls melancholy yearnings for other places. The "peaceful corner of earth," their old and lowly huts amid the birch trees, are infinitely dear to them, and they do not long "for another Eden." They are happy to remain in the villages and to be one there with nature and with their people.

> On the overflowed bank, beyond the river,
> The radiant day I shall greet
> With carefree songs of the village.
> Where the earth drinks from the quiet stream
> The fragrance of honey and rye,
> There in the crimson quiver of sunrise
> With thee, my people, I shall unite. . . . .
> —*Fomin.*

> Happy is he who lives in humble joy,
> Who has no friend nor foe,
> Who, passing along the village road,
> To the hayricks and stacks will pray. . . . .
> —*Essenin.*

While wandering along the "village road," where only an old cart at times drives by, a calm peace penetrates the peasant's heart. And in his complete resignation before God and His creation, Nature, his soul, filled with humble joy, prays to the wheat and haystacks.

When away from their dear "blue fields" and villages, the peasant poets seem out of place and forlorn. It is hard for them to adjust themselves to new surroundings. To their understanding the essence of all life is in the village; only there do they feel thoroughly at home and see the clear images of their mind's best thought. In the country they behold nature's grace, and their hearts discern in it "other joys and griefs."

> Again I behold the blue fields;
> The puddles wrinkle the sun's flushed cheeks.
> My heart has other joys and griefs,
> And to my tongue the new words cling.
> Peace be with ye, groves, meadows and lindens.
> —*Essenin.*
>
> My books I dropped on the grass,
> Amid the sparkling bright dew,
> Away my soul's fetters, away,
> The book of Life is around me again. . . . .
> —*Fomin.*
>
> Away from the cities
> I shall go into the fields, to the sun.
> From a cup of thy azure skies
> Give thy sacrament, O Earth!
> —*Idem.*

As soon as the peasant poets perceive again the fields and embrace in a glance the wide outstretched country before them, they immediately drop the books, the new thoughts and habits acquired in the cities, and feel once more in complete harmony with "Mother Nature." Under the emotion of love of earth, of the hospitable and familiar countryside, their souls free themselves from the fetters of the city, and "new words cling" to their tongues. Those are the words directly inspired by "the book of Life" around them. And with new exultation and rapture they sing again

> Of the fields drunk with vernal sun,
> Of the cranes crying in the skies,
> Of the golden sun glittering in the stream,
> Of the green reeds bathed in the river.
>
> —*Radimov.*

Thus the element of nature is manifest in all the peasant poets. Their songs to "Mother Nature" are stirring and impressive. Their feeling of awe and reverence carries with it a deep gratitude to God for His creation.

CHAPTER VI

THE ATTITUDE OF THE PEASANT POETS TOWARD THE CITY

O city, city! In a cruel combat
Thou hast christened us a carrion and a curse. . . . .
—Essenin.

In order to grasp and understand the spirit of contemporary Russia one must bear in mind the significant
fact that the peasants have no love, no sympathy, and no
good will, either for the city or for the proletariat. Numerous and varied are the causes of this attitude. Men who
jealously cherish a reverent feeling for the quiet village
and its mystical and patriarchal atmosphere; men who
constantly revel in the bright colors of the fields and the
country cannot be attracted by the confused noise and the
sooty sky of the industrial centers. The sinister silhouettes
of the big cities, the smoky aspect of the restless factories,
the huge machines with their hidden mechanism, are repulsive to the tillers of the soil. The rapid development of
the city's material luxury and the enthusiasm shown by
the city workers for the demoniac forces of the lathes and
machines have no fascination for the peasants. Having
always felt deeply the iron yoke of the city, which was
crushing them, the peasants look with great suspicion upon

all its elements, agencies, and forces. They are particularly afraid of the unfathomed discordances of passions, of the anarchy and chaos evolving therefrom. Thus, despite some purely external appearances that have deceived certain foreign observers, the peasants have no love for the city. On the contrary they despise it; its schemes, aims, and aspirations are absolutely foreign to them.

Along with this hostility toward the city the peasant poetry reveals a feeling of antagonism and of deep resentment against the urban workmen, whose minds, as we shall see, are indelibly impressed by iron and steel, by factories, furnaces, and machines, and by "cities of concrete" and of crowded humanity. The feeling of animosity between the peasants and the urban workmen is the more striking when one remembers that they all are of the same stock. For almost every city worker was originally a peasant, a tiller of the soil, a slave of the former landlord, a "carrion," a "curse." All of them suffered equally under the yoke of tsarism and all of them are opopressed now in different ways under the régime of the Bolsheviks. Yet there is no doubt that the gulf between these two social classes that have only recently appeared on the arena of their country's political life is daily becoming wider and deeper. And since the hostility of the peasants toward the city and the proletariat is now one of the most burning and pressing questions in Soviet Russia, it is already reflected in much of the popular poetry.

The root of the enmity between these two classes lies hidden in the depths of their contrasting outlook on life, of their psychology and their aspirations. The urban workmen, imbued as they are with the ideas of scientific socialism, consider themselves supermen, free-thinkers, ardent adherents of science, and worshipers of progress. In following the Marxian principle of class struggle they have become true communists in their temper, their spirit, and their aims. The peasants' spirit, on the other hand, is essentially individualistic. They have no sympathy for communism and are absolutely opposed to the gospel of Internationalism and to the socialistic system of economics. They still recognize the sacredness of private property and strongly support the principle of free trade. Besides, the peasants, as we have seen, continue to be attached to religion and to remain faithful to past traditions. Because of all this the city worker regards the peasant as ''carrion,'' as an ignorant, stupid, and inferior being who is continually hampering and obstructing the socialistic activities of the proletariat, and thus delaying the coming reign of Communism.

The discord between the two opposing camps, which is now threatening the whole system of the dictatorship of the Proletariat, reached its climax in May, 1918, when the Soviet government adopted the peculiar policy of ''Military Communism.'' This extraordinary measure consisted in prohibiting free trade in all commodities and in legalizing the use of armed force for the requisitioning of food in the villages. Owing to the Bolshevik policy of industrial nationalization and also to the civil war which was still raging throughout the whole country, production in the

cities had become completely paralyzed. The meagre sup-
plies of the government were exhausted; there was no food
for the town population and the Red Army. Exchange
between city and village had ceased. For, having stopped
production, the cities could not supply anything to the
villagers, who were naturally unwilling to give away their
produce for nothing. The peasants were in dire need of
various farm implements. Because the government could
not furnish these the peasants refused to feed the starving
cities. Thus the food question became one of the most
difficult problems of the Soviet leaders, who fancied that
they could solve it by establishing "Military Communism."
The peasants were now to hand over to the authorities
everything that they produced above their own needs. A
violent struggle ensued between the peasantry and the
special armed detachments that were sent to the villages
to carry out the new policy of the government. The "Food
Army" soon began to act in an arbitrary way, confiscating
not only the surplus of the peasants' produce, but even the
seed for next year's harvest. "The peculiarity of Military
Communism," wrote Lenin, "lay in this: that we actually
took away from the peasant his surplus of produce and
sometimes, even, a part of the stores that were absolutely
necessary to his existence." The armed detachments
treated the peasants as enemies and traitors and committed
great excesses in their attacks on the villages that resisted
them. These violent methods infuriated the villagers.
Regarding their stocks of grain and cattle as their private
property, they were in no mood to deliver them to the

"Food Army" for no other remuneration than promises to create a "communistic Eden." Risings spread in many provinces and, as Lenin recognized some time later, "the equilibrium between the proletariat and the peasantry was destroyed."

The policy of forced food requisitioning continued for about three years, but as it did not meet the problems of the Soviet government it had to be abandoned. Not being able to resist the armed detachments physically, the peasants retaliated in a more effective way. They reduced the acreage which they cultivated, killed their cattle, and destroyed great quantities of their products rather than deliver them to the "Food Army." This "passive resistance of the peasants," which was carried on, despite threats and decrees, with an indomitable stubbornness, with a tenacious, unbroken perseverance, forced the Soviet government to capitulate. The Bolsheviks had to admit that their policy of "Military Communism" and of the "sacred war for corn" was a mistake and a failure. Realizing that the drastic measures against the peasantry would be suicidal for the dictatorship of the Proletariat, Lenin bluntly came out for the New Economic Policy (NEP) and forced its acceptance in the spring of 1921.

This was the first receding step of the Communists and it was of the greatest significance. For it showed clearly that the peasant class was absolutely opposed to the suppression of free trade as well as to all the communistic dreams of the city workers. Note that it was the resistance of the peasantry that proved strong enough to break the attempt of the Soviet government to establish Communism in Russia. It was not the Allies, by their blockade, nor Kolchak, Denikin, Yudenich, and Wrangel with their "White Armies" that frustrated these bold communistic endeavors of the dictators of the Proletariat. This fact could not be denied even by the Bolshevik leaders. In the Tenth Assembly of the Communist party Lenin declared on March 15, 1921:

> We must realize that only by agreement with the peasantry can we save the socialistic revolution in Russia in view of the fact that it has not yet advanced into other countries. The peasants are dissatisfied with the present form of our relations with them. They do not want such relations and will not let them continue. This is indisputable. The peasants' will has been definitely expressed. We must reckon with it. We are sufficiently sober politicians to be able to speak our mind. Let us reconsider our policy toward the peasantry. Essentially our situation is as follows: We must either satisfy the peasants economically and allow freedom of exchange, or else we must maintain the power of the proletariat (i.e., the Communist Party) in Russia, which is impossible because of the delay of the International Revolution. Economically we cannot do this.

Another Bolshevik leader, Bukharin, while deploring the fact that the peasants were unable to grasp the idea of Communism, makes, in his "New Economic Policy of Soviet Russia," the following bitter confession:

> At the time of the November Revolution and previous to it we were the party that bade the peasant to kill the land-owner and take his land. The Bolsheviks were then thought to be capital fellows: they gave to the peasants everything and demanded nothing in return. But in the end we became the party which gave nothing and demanded everything from the peasants. They consequently turned against the communists, who were taking away their bread and who

furthermore were preaching absurd ideas of communism, unsuitable to the peasants.

While recognizing that the peasants' "proprietary instincts" were the cause of the New Economic Policy, Bukharin concludes with the hope that the Bolsheviks will ultimately succeed in "getting the better of the petty bourgeois tendencies." Meanwhile, with the New Economic Policy, capitalism and free trade had to come back.

Having won such important economic concessions, the peasants, becoming more and more conscious of their power, are beginning to think of freeing themselves from the political oppression of the dictatorship of the Proletariat. They know that Russia is primarily an agricultural country and not an industrial one. They therefore cannot see why the tillers of the soil, the organic, active force of the State, should be governed by a small minority. They do not want any longer to be treated like children. They believe they are able to take care of themselves without the spurious guardianship of the supreme, governing power of the Proletariat. They consider that the city workers are wrong in claiming that they alone have paid dearly for the revolution, and that they alone should therefore have the exclusive right of controlling the State. The peasants strongly resent such statements as that of Bukharin:

We are making economic concessions in order to avoid making political concessions. We shall agree to no coalition government nor to anything like it, not even equal rights to peasants and workers. We cannot do that. The concessions [economic] do not in any way change the class character of the dictatorship.

Owing to this dictatorial attitude of the Proletariat the animosity between the two classes is growing stronger and the struggle between them is far from losing its intensity. Small wonder that many Soviet officials, realizing the seriousness and gravity of this situation, are trying to unite the two opposing camps. But up to the present the results have been negligible. For it is utterly impossible to transform the peasants into communists and to do away with the individualistic ideology to which they firmly cling.

There was a time when the Russian city workers and the peasants felt that they were united by common interests. That time is gone and the close contact between city and village is severed. The tillers of the soil and the factory laborers seem now to have very little in common. They present two very distinct social strata whose different characteristics are well emphasized in the following lines of the talented peasant poet Kluyev:

> We are from the land of rye and oats,
> Of chintz and rusticity;
> You—from that of iron and concrete,
> Of splendor and electricity.
>
> We are fire, water, pastures,
> Sun and bread, and winter corn,
> You can tell us no mysteries
> Of the fragrant garden.
>
> Your songs are the groans of the hammer;
> Their tune is dross and tin:
> Your tree of life is a broken limb,
> It bears no fruit but heads.
>
> . . . .

On the proletarian altar
The owls came to build their nests . . . .
Your blood is diluted with water
From the paper stream.[2] . . . .

We are from the land of rye and oats,
And know the magic words
By which the stormy wings
Will carry you toward our world.

There in a hut the reed-pipe
Echoes the peacock's cry . . . .
The buckwheat genius
In new Russia will flourish. . . . .

With subtle intuition and poetic insight the peasant poets perceive the divergence between their mode of thought and that of the workmen. They realize clearly that "the land of rye and oats" is very different, if not altogether opposed, to that of "electricity, iron and concrete." For the simplicity of rustic life weaves fancies which are in sharp conflict with the laws of science. The peasant poets identify themselves with the elements; they are "fire, water, and sun." Living far away from the artificialities created by city civilization, being nearer to nature than the city workers, they imagine that they are also nearer to the truth of life. They know that the factory toiler cannot reveal to them "the mysteries of the fragrant garden." And it is exactly these mysteries, revealed to the peasants in the rustle of grass, in the entire symphony of nature, that are of vital importance to them.

---

[2] That is, of communistic pamphlets.

Mother Nature always stirs up in their hearts a variety of
emotions and they cannot but feel her throbbing pulse.
In "the groans of the hammer" and in "the dross and
tin" the magical freshness of life disappears; the mysterious workings of nature are felt no more, something is
destroyed forever, the "tree of life is a broken limb" and
"it bears no fruit but heads." The cool-headed adherents
of exact science lack that pulse of elemental life which
the peasants feel so intensely. Therefore the latter believe
that the blood of the city workers is "diluted with water,"
that it possesses no force and that its reaction to life is
weak.

There is always a genuine pathos in the peasant poets
when they speak of the "mystery," the beauty, and the
silent charm of their world—the village. A unique world
it is, for nothing is so dear to their hearts and so near to
their souls. And yet the domineering city tries to crush
and wipe it out.

> The world of mystery, my ancient world,
> Like the wind thou art calm and silent.
> Thine aged throat is strangled
> By the strong hand of the pavement.
>
> —*Essenin.*

The peasants revolt against the brutal force of the city,
against the encroachments upon the fields of the "telegraph poles" which destroy the beauty and the soul of
their Mother Nature.

Unsuspected powers have been awakened in the peasants since the revolution. They are now on a higher intel-

lectual level than they were before. They have obtained
good training in their fight with the city, and they begin
to understand better the politics of the dictatorship of the
Proletariat. The conflict of interests is now such that
either the peasants or the city workers must rule. And it
is more than probable that the "buckwheat genius" will
ultimately become the master of New Russia.

Chapter VII

ORIGIN AND DEVELOPMENT OF PROLETARIAN POETRY IN RUSSIA

Step aside, the workman is coming, get off the pavements,
Make way for him—the present Dante.   —*Filipchenko.*

We live for a different beauty; we are free, we are brave.
                                        —*Kirillov.*
We are winged impetuosity,
We are all powerful, we can do everything.   —*Sadofiev.*

The Proletarian poets, with all their bewildering variety
of revolutionary themes, and with their equally bewildering yearnings for a communistic state, present a striking
contrast to the poets of foregoing generations. In almost
all the prerevolutionary Russian poets we have an in-
grained abhorrence of unruly disorder; we find liberty
fenced in by laws, veneration of past traditions. We find
in their works a belief in the gradual betterment of human
ills, a hatred of political fanaticism, a distrust of the violent
methods and sweeping theories that are so much in vogue
with the extreme and resolute proletarian bards. The
poets of the old régime were never of sanguine temperament. Their reflective minds were always apt to be dark-
ened by the apprehension of the consequences of a fierce
fight. With few exceptions those poets represented the

opinions of educated liberals on political, social, and religious questions. Rioting and violent radicalism merely strengthened their feeling of the widespread distress, of the privations and grievances of the whole Russian nation.

The works of the proletarian poets are of quite a different temper. The spirit of fierce revolt, of continuous combat, of destruction, of mob-rule runs through all their poems. Their poetry gives us no such delicate, esthetic pleasure as is found in the works of their predecessors. It is rather a poetry of excitement, of nervous tension, tinged with fever. It is not written for quiet, gentle spirits, but for the restless crowd, which likes loud and resonant words. In vain would one look in it for the usual qualities of correct taste and polished diction. Wishing to speak to the multitude, the proletarian poets have completely done away with both the outward and the inward media employed by earlier Russian poets. Their aim is not the quest for beauty, order, melody, technical poetic excellence, suppleness and flexibility of language. They strive only to give direct and simple expression to the mob passions that are generated amid modern social conditions in Russia. They are not at all concerned with the highest heights and the deepest depths of the prerevolutionary poetry. They ridicule the mystic and dreaming spirit of the Russian symbolists, their passion for grasping the secret voice of the universe. The proletarian bards have discovered a new source of inspiration, a new pathos, in the bestial and tameless strength of the Socialist revolution. Their prevailing spirit is inspired by the will of this revolution to

create from the present materialistic age itself a passion
that cannot be held down, that must carry the multitude
with it, no matter how brutal and repugnant that passion
may seem. In their poetic activity the proletarian poets
have a definite program and a clear objective for attack.
They proclaim the destruction of capitalism in all its
aspects. This theme forms the block and the statue, the
pigments and the canvas of their artistic creations. They
are still governed and possessed by the idea of a world
revolution, and they continue to sing it with a pertinacity
that refuses to be daunted.

A poetry with such a new pathos could be created only
by men who sought to impose their ideas and their feelings
upon others. That the proletarian poets are such men, will
be sufficiently manifest from their poems.

Proletarian poetry appeared in Russia immediately
after the revolution of 1905. Long before the end of the
disastrous Russo-Japanese war, both the intellectuals and
the workingmen had been clamoring for social reforms.
And when defeat in the war came to stamp the autocracy
with the brand of corruption and inefficiency, the government of Nicholas II was forced to grant a Constitution to
the people. The city workingmen obtained at that time
freedom of the press and the right to organize labor unions.
Each union began to edit its own newspaper or magazine,
in which, besides articles on professional subjects, were also
published verses written by factory workers. Up to 1914
the poems of the proletarian poets dealt exclusively with
the themes of class struggle, exploitation, and oppression.

They were nothing but socialistic appeals against capitalism and the tsaristic régime. There was no real poetry in these verses; their authors possessed little or no talent, and very few of them had any notion about the technique of poetry.

Yet the first productions of these poets satisfied the demands of the awakened factory workers as no prerevolutionary literature had satisfied them. This was mainly due to the fiery protest voiced in this poetry against the heartless way in which the government was then treating their fellow-workers. It will be remembered that the years 1906–1914 were a period of the darkest reaction in Russia. Soon after the Tsar's manifesto of October 17, 1905, the government started to take vengeance on all those who had previously participated in the movement for liberation. Thousands were arrested and exiled. The "houses of the dead," the prisons of the Empire, were filled to capacity. The Constitution granted in 1905 was gradually explained away and soon lost all its meaning. The result of this reaction was the decision of the workingmen that the tsaristic régime must at all costs be overthrown. And in June, 1914, just before the world war, about four hundred thousand Petrograd workers went out on a political strike, and revolution was once more in the air in the streets of the Russian capital.

The need then felt by all the Russian workingmen of a new and courageous utterance was completely satisfied by the few proletarian poets. Risking their lives they sang the glory of the fight with the evil forces of the government.

They tried to show in their poems that the proletariat was not exhausted from this battle, as were most of the intellectuals. They proclaimed to their fellow-workingmen that they alone were "the power of the near future" and "the Messiah of tomorrow." The factory workers felt in those verses their own thought, their own aim, will, and energy. It was the note which their first poets struck, much more than the form and the verbose style in which they expressed their ideas, that appealed so much to them. And it was this note that secured for the new poets almost immediately the enthusiastic admiration of the whole Russian proletariat.

It must be stated, however, that in the first period of their poetic activity, from 1905 to 1914, the proletarian poets were yet at school. Even the best among them were mere schoolboys writing exercises on the successes and disappointments of the revolution of 1905. With the year 1914 a new period begins for the proletarian muse, the period of apprenticeship. It lasted till 1920 and certain good results came of it, thanks to the valuable counsel which the new poets received from Maxim Gorky. This popular Russian writer, who had always taken a great interest in workingmen and their cause, became in 1914 particularly interested in their literary productions. I say "particularly" because already in 1905, when Gorky founded the first "legal" socialist daily in Russia, *The New Life,* he had invited a number of factory workers to collaborate for that newspaper. And in 1906, when Gorky left Russia, he continued to correspond from abroad with the most gifted proletarian prose writers and poets, trying to help them in every possible way. In 1909, while living in Capri, Italy, Gorky took part in the foundation of a Social Democratic School for Russian workingmen who were forced to leave their native country on account of their political ideas. Though the main aim of this school was to prepare socialist propagandists, Gorky nevertheless paid great attention to the literary pursuits of some of his pupils. Upon his return to Russia at the end of 1913, hundreds of proletarian poems began to reach him for his criticism and advice. Out of four hundred and fifty such poems, Gorky picked out about ninety and, on the eve of the war, published them under the title, *Our Songs*. This book was the first anthology of proletarian poetry in Russia. In an effort to encourage the new bards and to help them with his personal advice Gorky himself wrote a preface to *Our Songs*. As an illustration of the faith which Gorky then had in the new poets it will be worth while to quote a passage from it. There is nothing, I think, in which Gorky as a defender of proletarian literature is more characteristic than the following lines:

Written by your comrades, this book is a new and significant event in our life. It eloquently tells of the growth of the intellectual power of the proletariat. You, of course, understand very well that, aside from his lack of leisure, the workingman-writer, in relating his impressions vividly and accurately, that is to say, artistically, is hampered by his slight skill in the use of the pen, the writer's tool; he is handicapped by his unfamiliarity with literary technique, and his greatest obstacle is his lack of words—his inability to choose amidst a score of them the simplest, the best. But in spire of all these difficulties, it seems to me that you may still say without exaggeration, that this book of yours is interesting and that herein is something to cause you joy. There is no doubt that this little book will be duly recognized as one of the first attempts of the Russian proletariat to create its own artistic literature. ''Fancy!''—some one will say to me with mistrust—''never and nowhere has such literature existed!'' But, many a thing that now exists, has never been before; previously there has been no working class such as we now have, with such a spiritual content as in these present days. I am absolutely convinced that the proletariat is able to create its own artistic literature, just as it has produced with great effort and enormous sacrifices its daily press.

There is much truth in these words of Gorky. The poems which we find in *Our Songs* show that the Russian workingmen are men of great ambition, which must naturally go before great achievement. Who will doubt that Gorky was right in asserting that the factory workers had made considerable intellectual progress when he had before him such lines as these, from the poem dedicated by the young proletarian poet Trifonov to those enthusiastic workers who fell in their fight against the government:

> So proudly unconcerned, with a smile in their eyes,
> To death and torment—as to a feast—they went;
> In dark prisons, through years of bondage
> They have kept their faith unstained.
>
> They have forgotten their own suffering,
> Dreaming of happiness for their native land.
> Neither exile nor despair, nor years of absence
> Could kill their faith and love.
> —*Trifonov.*

Another poet, Bogdanov, reminding his fellow-workingmen of what was already past, the revolution of 1905, writes thus on the reaction that followed it:

THE PAST

Trust not the days of calm, of pause and silence,
Colorless, wearisome and bitter as deceit!
While the open wounds still bleed
The past will not die, no indeed . . . .
But through death-like fog it will lure into the distance.
Oh, hast thou guessed
How in the stifled peace of homeless poverty,
In the iron gnashing of wakeful factory,
And in the crowd, hiding old dreams and distress,
The anger and might'of the enslaved people had ripened?
O, hast thou heard
From disastrous conflagrations, from desolate fields,
From cemeteries overgrown with hungry crosses,
From heavens o'ercast with the sadness of brothers' tears,
The approaching breath of threatening storms?
Trust not the days of calm, of pause and silence;
They are deceitful, like a dream at twilight.
Under the sacrificial ashes the past did not die . . . .
The people is not conquered;
In prisons it sharpens the sacred swords. . . . .

—Bogdanov.

Gorky was not mistaken in saying that *Our Songs* will have to be mentioned in any history of the development of proletarian literature. In that anthology we already find poems of Gastev, Gerassimov, Ionov, Kirilov, Filipchenko, and others who are counted among the most prominent contemporary proletarian poets. Gorky's encouragement filled all of them with enthusiasm, and their subsequent works show that he was not altogether wrong in saluting them, in 1914, as the rising stars of Soviet Russia.

After the revolution of 1917 Gorky continued to be the guiding spirit of the proletarian bards, and as a result of his activity there appeared in 1917 and 1918 several other anthologies in which many poems of distinction are to be found.

In 1918, a new cultural organization sprang up in the industrial centers of Russia under the name of *Proletkult* ("Proletarian Culture"). On the advice of Gorky it soon began the publication of many literary reviews, devoting scores of pages to the question of the technique of writing prose and poetry. This organization also founded a number of "Studios" where the factory workers might receive literary training. In 1919 many books of verse written by workingmen were published. It is evident from these verses that the "Studios" of the Proletkult have done good work. For in this poetry one already notes the gift of terse and forcible expression and the turn for apt metaphors that comes from a lively imagination. The Soviet government, of which Gorky was at that time still an official, encouraged the new proletarian muse by providing the most talented poets with the leisure necessary for artistic work. It goes without saying that all of them belonged to the Bolshevik party and sang, as they still do, the glory and beauty of the new communistic age.

The third period of the proletarian muse began in 1920, when the best poets of the Moscow Proletkult left that organization and formed their own group, the *Kuznitsa* ("Smithy"), which became the voice, almost the incarnation of the Soviet régime. In 1920 there were still in

Russia a few "bourgeois" prose writers and poets who could not be silent. There were also many *Poputchiki* ("fellow-travelers"), that is, writers who were not at all inclined to accept all the theories of the Bolsheviks, who were in essence anti-communists. At that time even the contemporary peasant poets began to be looked upon with contempt by the proletarian poets. The latter saw in the peasant poetry a "bourgeois character." By 1920, as we have seen, the wild enthusiasm of the peasants for the revolution had passed away. Their vague hatred of their former enemies, the "bourgeois," had been toned down into warnings and demands for reasonable improvements in their ruined country. The poets of the "Kuznitsa" pictured this literary situation as one extremely dangerous. They therefore felt that if Russia was to have a "real proletarian" literature, a class poetry, they alone must strike out a new path for her. Was not the promised land of the Bolshevik régime a new communistic world? Was not the old bourgeois culture now to be thought of with contempt and be altogether discarded and forgotten? Could one doubt that a new era in art, literature, and learning was to come forthwith? The *bourgeoisie* and the anti-revolutionaries might be skeptical about all these things, but not the pillars of the dictatorship of the Proletariat. In order to set forth their views on poetry and art, the poets of the *Kuznitsa* founded a magazine bearing the same name, in which they enunciated their Credo.

Few poetical schools have been so prodigal of manifestoes as the *Kuznitsa* group. In the first one, published in their magazine in 1920, we find the following declaration:

For the organization of its forces in the social field, in struggle and reconstruction, the proletariat must have its own class art. The spirit of this art is the industrial collectivism. It perceives the universe and reflects it from the viewpoint of industrial collectivism, expressing the relation of its emotions, and its militant and creative will. . . . .

Yesterday we were forging the new life, the life of Matter,—in the foundry,—today we are endeavoring to create its new content in graceful and vivid word images. And just as in the foundry a new form can be better and more quickly welded out of raw material, if one knows when and how to strike, so in the art of poetry we must acquire a steady hand in the technical means and methods of a higher order; only then shall we mould our thoughts and feelings into an original proletarian poetry.

This conception of art and poetry seems, to say the least, too narrow and too startling, inasmuch as one is not inclined to believe that there can be such a thing as a class poetry. Poetry is concerned with the life, strivings, and emotions of all human beings, without any class distinctions. A real poet is never animated by class sentiment, but by the faith and the feelings which are common to the soul of all men, of the *bourgeois* as well as of the proletarian. All individuals, no matter to which social class they belong, experience great emotions of love and hatred, of joy and sorrow. All human beings are moved by kindness and sympathy. *Bourgeois,* peasants, and proletarians, all can be great in courage, endurance, in hope, and in profound despair. A sunrise, oceans and rivers, mountains and plains, forests and fields, gardens and flowers can speak and appeal to all classes of society. But the proletarian poets do not wish to take this simple truth into consideration. They want to be the singers of only one class, their own.

In giving us a class conception of poetry, the *Kuznitsa* poets seemed at least to recognize that they had as yet, in 1920, achieved less profound results than the prerevolutionary Russian poets. They had yet, as they admitted, to "acquire a steady hand in the technical means and methods of a higher order," for creating "an original proletarian poetry." But in their second Manifesto of 1921 they grew bolder. They believed that they had already created a "monumental art" and produced a poetry "capable of developing into a great universal and human art for life, and for the very existence and growth of a harmonious and beautiful human being. . . . ."

In reality there was in 1921 nothing yet worthy of special note in the poetry of the proletarians. Still, in their simplicity they believed that they could already disassociate themselves completely from all the former tendencies in art and literature. Symbolism, Futurism, and Imagism must be done away with, because these literary and artistic schools reflected an age and an ideology which were too different from their own:

Symbolism was born of the fear of the revolution of tomorrow felt by the decaying *bourgeois* society. It always signifies a defense, a safeguard, and never an offense. Like a monk in his cell, it hates and worships simultaneously.

Futurism grew out of the extreme, hypertrophically developed individualism of the intelligentsia of the years just preceding its fall. Futurism meant death; the future of it was only decay. To go forward meant for it to go toward its own peril; to stand still was to intrench itself in the fortress of technique and all sorts of sophistry. For retreat there was no room. . . . .

Imagism is a manifestation of the mortal agony of a *petit-bourgeois* society which has time only for analogies and for incoherent imagery of happenings. . . . .''

The proletarian poets are great masters at negation. They are really "brave," and "can do everything," particularly condemn and reject everyone who does not share their narrow and utopian idea of a "proletarian art." In their blindness they cannot realize how vital and progressive was the work of the Symbolists, Futurists, and Imagists in the field of Russian art and literature. In their vagaries of political excitement they cannot estimate with unbiased judgment even their immediate predecessors in poetry. Leaving out of account all that is of sterling worth in the poetry of former Russian poets, the bards of the *Kuznitsa* come to the sage conclusion that:

Yesterday's art of expression has degenerated into a universal deformity and is unable to touch the industrial class, just as the hand of a corpse cannot reach out to the living.

Therefore the "forgers of a new beauty" raise their voices and "lifting the Red Flag," pompously declare:

We are raising the workingman's hammer in order to wall up the door of this dreadful "chamber"; we are hammering down the last nail on the lid of this embellished sepulcher of art.

Having thus with one heavy blow of their hammer destroyed, in 1921, all the former schools of poetry, the forgers of the *Kuznitsa* bethought themselves that something new must be erected. It was easy enough to reject all the *bourgeois* art, and to shout:

Step aside, the workman is coming, get off the pavements,
Make way for him—the present Dante.

Such bombastic utterances must suggest to their readers the poverty of the real achievements in poetry that lay behind them. Besides, some of their opponents began to point out to the admirers of the *Kuznitsa,* and not without reason, that they were inconsistent; that many of the things which they condemned in the prerevolutionary poets were exactly what they enjoyed in the "present Dantes." The innovators were rather slow in seeing this. In 1923, however, in an effort to give their final viewpoint on the art of the future and on proletarian poetry, they published a third Manifesto, which they consider their most constructive utterance. Affirming that "the changes in the forms of society determine the type of art," and that "art is as necessary to the proletariat as an army, transportation, factories, and foundries, this Manifesto continues:

Proletarian art is nothing but a prism in which the countenance of a class is focussed, a mirror in which the workingmen see themselves, the things past and accomplished, those which are being created, and those to come.

Therefore the aim of the proletarian artist must be:

1. To be conscious of, and to present the image of the creator of the communistic society, that is, the proletariat.
2. To forge the revolutionary character of the New Man.
3. By means of words—the workingman's tool,—to plough the fallow land on which this New Man will grow the new conditions of life (that is, "to show the new ways of living," "the red society").
4. To demonstrate this new way of living not cinematographically, not heartlessly, but to pierce it with a shower of emotions and thoughts, to install accumulators for storing the wills and consciousnesses which, though scattered, already belong to the life of revolutionary construction.

5. To produce artistic images of the scientific Marxian revolutionary viewpoint.
6. To destroy through artistic works the *bourgeois* ideology of
   the inherited emotions of a primitive property holder.
7. To sum up the results of the revolution.
8. To outline the paths of the future.

Such were the viewpoint and the aims of the proletarian
Kuznitsa poets in 1923, and such they remain to this day.

It is not hard to discern that the principles expressed
in the Manifesto of 1923 were essentially the same as those
enunciated in 1920 and in 1921. The idea that the proletarian poet should become the interpreter and the propa-
gator of the communistic age did not originate with the
poets of the *Kuznitsa*. All that can be said of this Manifesto of 1923 is that its authors reveal here more clearly
than in their previous manifestoes the inner meaning of
their thought. The "present Dante" must try to inculcate
Marxian ideas and create a passion of revolt against the
tyranny of the "*bourgeois* ideology." Thus he will "forge
the revolutionary character of the new man" who will
destroy the old world and become the creator of the new
one.

The poet's material is to be "the whole range of the
ordinary and common life of the workingmen." This pre-
determines the form of the poet's creation. They must be
adapted to one another and become synthetically united:
"The elements of creative material and the rudiments of
rhythm and composition must be an organic unity."

But above all the new poetry must serve the interest
of the proletarian class. It should not be a mood of the

poet's own. The communistic age has developed a new kind of sensibility, a collective brotherhood and feeling, which demand a new kind of poetry, an art "according to its own image and likeness."

A class of collective unanimity, of universal brotherhood, industrial fellowship in labor, struggle and defeat; a class of common interests, feelings, emotions—from practical trifles to lofty flights toward the summits of ideals; a class—a monolith which history has cut into a monument of Memnon, announcing the dawn of the new day: such a class must create art only according to its own image and likeness. . . . .

It must be added that the same thoughts were less vividly expressed by other proletarian poets, particularly by the *October* group founded in 1922. The main purpose of the *Octobrists* was to wage a bitter warfare against "the intellectual and ideological poets" and to preserve "the orthodox purity," the most extreme tendencies, of proletarian poetic art.

But in so far as the conception of poetry and the rôle of the poet are concerned there is really no difference between the *October,* the *Kuznitsa* and other groups. As a matter of fact all the proletarian poets without any exception understand alike the function of poetry and their own vocation. The basic tendency of all consists in their endeavor "to systematize and organize life by means of word, in the Marxian conception." And their sole aim in art is the re-shaping of life in conformity with the requirements of the Bolshevik revolution. All of them are to create a poetry which is not to adorn life, not a poetry of mood, where the individual element predominates, but a poetry of rational thought, in which the individual elements perish in favor of collectivism.

Such is, in brief, the history of the proletarian poetry in Russia, in the development of which Gorky, as we have seen, played a very prominent part.

The attempt of the Russian factory workers to create a poetry of their own presents a curious phenomenon in the world's literature. Having become through force of circumstances the only ruling political party in Russia, the city proletarians intend to change not only the political and economic structure of the state, but also its cultural development. They wish to create their own culture, which shall differ in every respect from the *bourgeois* culture, and which shall express exclusively the workingman's ideology of life. Intoxicated with the revolution and with political victory, there are no limits to their daring. They believe, in their simplicity, that it is possible to create at will something out of nothing in the field of art, and they are striving to do away with "bourgeois poetry," with the themes, forms, and tendencies of all the prerevolutionary Russian poets. In their persistent negation of everything they have come to deny even the importance of the Russian literary treasures in which so many different shades of thought, so many aspirations of the human soul, have found artistic expression. The proletarian poets, having destroyed much, are now striving to create a new beauty, a new faith, a new god. Whether or not they will succeed in their endeavors is still for the future to decide.

CHAPTER VIII

ATTITUDE OF THE PROLETARIAN POETS TOWARD THE REVOLUTION

> Today there are red carnations in our souls,
> There are iron and granite in our muscles today. . . . .
> *—Alexandrovsky.*

> Today
> The last ladders
> And the bridges of the Past are burnt.
> Today
> The weakest
> Is the power in a free land. . . . .
> *—Bezymensky.*

> Today, workmen, the Earth, all the Earth,
> Crimsoning on the streets and paths,
> Discards the black blouse of night,
> And echoing with our songs now rings. . . . .
> *—Obradovich.*

The "today" to which the proletarian poets sing their hymns was November the seventh, 1917. On that day the social revolution in Russia was no longer a symbol, an idea—it was an accomplished fact. The theories of the Russian city proletariat concerning its political supremacy had been realized. On that day "the ladders and bridges of the Past" were burnt, and the weakest became the strongest. That day indeed made the urban workers what the tsars had been of old: the power, the masters, the dictators of the state. And this newborn reality of the working class gave to all the proletarian poets the greatest joy and happiness that life can bestow. It kindled them with a blazing fire whose flames grew exceedingly hot and red. On that autumn day there were "red carnations" in their souls, "fire and spring" in their gaze, "iron and granite" in their muscles. Their "bosoms quivered with a passionate might," and

> Everyone was a head taller,
> Everyone was brave and strong. . . . .
> —*Kirillov.*

These new sensations called for a new poetry which was to fashion the very soul of the revolution and vibrate in unison with its feverish rhythm. The songs of the proletarians were now to be

> A rebellious call, a clear peal, masterful, red,
> A mighty call to sun, life, and struggle;
> To wicked and wearisome fate they are a proud and angry
>   challenge. . . . .   —*Kirillov.*

Thus, amid the din and the horrors of the great social upheaval they began to sing Hosanna to the revolution.

> Great is she, born in serfdom,
> Amidst fetters, grief, and oppression;
> Amidst people whose life, like the night, is dark
> From blood and tears, sweat and work.
>
> Beloved, radiant, she came
> On the gloomy days of the people's tempest,
> And swept away all curse and shame,
> Soaring like a whirlwind into the heavens.

Victorious, into dust she turned all,
With her impertinent, masterful hand;
On the ashes and ruins of bonfires
She builds for us a new and beautiful world. . . . .

—Shkulev.

There are days more stately than centuries:
Sparkle my song, and burn!
The autumn day is illumined
By the light of an immortal dawn. . . . .

—Kirillov.

Of a sudden, like a magic dream,
A dream of May flowers,
Came to us with healing power
Dazzlingly beautiful Freedom. . . . .

—Nechayev.

Animated with the faith that the revolution "swept away all curse and shame" and brought with it the "dazzlingly beautiful Freedom," the proletarian poets give play to their emotions and express their happiness with boundless exuberance. Again and again, with incessantly renewed joy, they recur to the theme of their victory, of their enthusiasm for the new age, of their greatest experience. Every one of them feels that he must celebrate the proletarian triumph with the highest intensity of his emotion.

The flowers of Revolt will set the world astir,
And moments into eternity will turn.
The flowers of Revolt will awaken the strings of the lyre,
Breathing into them inspiration and life.

And, like the tocsin of future beauty,
In the purple flames of turbulent revolt
They will strew the rainbow flowers
Of Renascence and Liberty. . . . .   *—Pomorsky.*

> Let your spirit be young forever,
> Like the foaming surf of the ocean;
> Over yonder on the Red Banner
> The sickle and the hammer shine like the sun. . . . .
>   —*Samobytnik.*
>
> Rise, ye brothers; rise, ye sisters!
> To the ranks, ye steel-tempered fighters!
> The light of the Future's Sun
> Already shines on the banner of crimson.   —*D. Bedny.*

The same tone and the same ardor run through all their songs. Their sadness, melancholy, and dejection of yesterday seem to have disappeared forever. Now they are gay, happy, and courageous. And since their "Day" has come, since the social revolution, dimly foreseen by only a few prophets, and clearly foretold by none, "of a sudden came with a healing power"; since "the earth trembled with a victorious hymn," the world to them is full of beauty. They all now hunger for life, because they already see "the light of the Future's Sun on the banner of crimson." The momentous change makes them want to live and gives them a zest for life.

> Enchanted with the chorus of sounds,
> Toward the sun, sea, hills, toward freedom I flee. . . . .
> Bright happiness and joy I desire. . . . .
>   —*Sadofiev.*

All things that of old had seemed to them cold and dead—the machine, the factory, the city—now appear as creators of the "workmen's palace" and of "future happiness." Everything is creation now. The brilliant electric signboards and advertisements, the tower, the belfry, the foundry, the furnace—everything is "incessantly creating

the workingmen's paradise.'' And a festival, a pleasure
breaks out of this idea of the bright future.

> The masses are on the square. The festival. The tumult.
>   The joy.
> The beloved brothers and sisters in their meeting rejoice.
>   . . . .
> ''Friends, towards the zenith, forward!
> Sing! Let the song peal and thunder!
> The band plays. The drums beat.
> The trumpets triumphantly blare.
> The boisterous tocsin is raging—
> Its brass is inviting
> And calling.
> The band plays. The drums beat.
> The trumpets triumphantly blare.   —*Malashkin.*

> Call each other
> And get together
> For joy and play. . . . .
> The tambourines jingle
> And the bugles ring—
> The sounds are sharp, coarse, free;
> They whirl clouds, living clouds;
> They are forging rapture, are forging the sounds.

> The trumpets blare;
> Like fiery manes float the banners;
> They flutter in the air;
> The gust hampers their turbulent ardor
> At the crimson hour when everywhere darkness is driven
>   away,
> Ready for the festival—loving and beautiful—the world
>   has risen.   —*Filipchenko.*

Thus they lavish themselves joyously on everything around
them, and feel that it is a real bliss to be alive at such a
time.

If one is to understand the workingmen's enthusiasm
for the revolution, it must be kept in mind that under the
old régime their life had been "like the night dark." The
industrial development of the country, begun on a large
scale in the nineties of the last century, was not accompanied by suitable labor legislation, which might have set
free the urban workers from their "fetters, grief, and
oppressions." And for decades hosts of them were gripped
in the chains of industrial slavery, and were forced to go

> Through prisons, chasms, and dreary days,
> Trampling over darkness and pain. . . . .
> —*Obradovich.*

It is true enough that the exploitation of the working
class has been very severe in Russia. Long hours, inade-
quate wages, poor housing accommodations in the large
industrial centers have doomed them to poverty and to
infinite suffering.

> Mines, factories, foundries
> Have maimed us and bent . . . .
> Capital's cursed burden
> Has doomed us to torment. . . . .
>
> Those at whose will we perished
> Left us no bread, but promised—
> The grace of Heaven
> On the Last Day of Judgment. . . . .   —*D. Bedny.*

From childhood they had "to sweat and to work" in
suffocating factories, and were absolutely cut off from the
sun and from the joys of the world. Small wonder that
we now hear them cry in their songs: "the sun is ours,"
"the sun shines for us," and the like.

For three hundred days not seeing the sun,
For three hundred days not seeing ourselves,
Now on a spring day brighter than the golden sun
We have come out into the open. . . . .

Upon our hearts knocks the sun;
The sun has arisen, the sun has arisen,
Its rays will warm
The old and the young. . . . .   —*Filipchenko.*

Time is the greatest teacher. In the past, when ignorance among the Russian masses was general, when all the peasants and most of the city workers were enslaved; when industrial enterprise, due to the economic conditions of the country, could not thrive, only a few of the proletarians felt their personal, individual worth. But with the emancipation of 1861, with the wider spread of education, with the growth of industry on an extensive scale, the sense of personal dignity and freedom grew stronger and stronger among the multitudes of the proletariat. These soon learned enough to contrast their miserable lot with the welfare of their employers. And it did not take them long to realize that their poverty, together with the political conditions of the country, was destroying their freedom, inner and outward alike. They became "tired of living in twilight" and longed passionately for a normal existence, consistent with full liberty of soul. Deprived of a free press and unable publicly to raise their voice in protest against their abnormal conditions, they pleaded with their employers and prayed to be freed from the "grievous bondage," from the wrongs and evils inherent in their dependence and privation. Again and again they reiterated their grievances to the government requesting that some steps be taken against the arbitrary will of their masters. But their pleas and complaints were ignored and they continued to suffer.

> The poison of insult and the bile of torment
> Oppressed our souls like lead.
> Raising our arms towards the skies
> Our grievous bondage we cursed. . . . .
>
> We waited, too long we waited
> Under the yoke of darkness and dread;
> We prayed, complained and wept
> And froze in winter's cold. . . . .
> —*Nechayev*.

Conscious of the fact that they deserved a brighter and happier lot, the workingmen made, on January 9, 1905, a direct appeal to Nicholas II, himself. In their petition to the Tsar, they wrote:

. . . . We have become beggars, we have been oppressed; we are burdened by toil beyond our powers; we are scoffed at; we are not recognized as human beings; we are treated as slaves who must suffer their bitter fate and who must keep silence. We suffered, but we are pushed farther into the den of beggary, lawlessness, and ignorance. We are choked by despotism and irresponsibility, and we are breathless. We have no more power, Sire; the limit of patience has been reached. There has arrived for us that tremendous moment when death is better than the continuation of intolerable torture. We have left off working, and we have declared to our masters that we will not begin to work until they comply with our demands. We beg but little; we desire only that without which life is not life, but only hard labor and eternal torture.

The workingmen of St. Petersburg accompanied by their wives and children marched toward the Winter Palace singing "God Save the Tsar." But their "Little Father" wished neither to see them nor to listen to their petition. They were met by a volley of bullets and hundreds of them were killed and wounded. Thus, instead of giving their sympathy and cooperation to the legal efforts of the workers, which would have led toward beneficient results, the "higher spheres" preferred to adopt such measures as lead to despair and revolt. They were blinded and could see no other way but that of implacable reaction. This uncompromising attitude of the government of Nicholas II toward social readjustments proved to be too costly to Russia, to the Romanovs themselves, and to all their subjects. It played the most conspicuous part in producing the state of mind that became so receptive to the Marxian principles. Degraded in body and mind, socially crushed and poverty-stricken, the workingmen faced a dilemma: either to continue to submit to social wrongs or to rise and blot them out in a desperate duel. At first they hesitated and could not decide which road to take. Finally, after reflection, they came to the bitter realization that struggle was necessary, that "death is better than the continuation of intolerable torture."

> Two roads before me branched:
> To go toward the Past, or toward the Future . . . .
> I hesitated, for many days could not decide,
> I wondered which one was more happy and bright.
> And having thought it over—I took
> The second, the road toward the Future . . . .
> Thus I went toward Struggle, Freedom, into the distance,
>   forward!
> > *—Sadofiev.*

It was the event of January 9, 1905, that changed the workingmen's state of mind. They lost all respect for the Tsar and their faith in the government was broken. The Socialist movement, hitherto confined to small groups, now began to affect large masses. The followers of Marx, the Social Democrats, now found in the workingmen's circles a new and favorable field for the propaganda of their ideas. The proletarians were soon convinced of the fact that the wrongs which oppressed and saddened their life sprang from the existing industrial system and they became a unit in demanding the abolition of private property, the establishment of community ownership of all raw materials, all machinery, all factories. All agencies of distribution—railways, canals, steamships, telegraphs, post offices, and the like—they wished now to own in common. They urged that production be regulated by consumption, and that equal hours of work be the measure of rewards. Society, they were assured, would thereby transform itself. Castes would disappear, poverty and its consequent evil results would cease, vices and "the chains of ages" would vanish forever. The Social Democrats inflamed the workingmen's brains with the idea of class struggle and nothing now could stop the city proletariat from fighting against the old order of things.

> Degraded and imprisoned,
> We have boldly sworn to fight. . . . .
> —D. Bedny.
> We are tired of living in twilight!
> We have awakened, arisen;
> We have waited too long for the fight,
> For the young life we are yearning.

> Vanish impotent fear!
> Steady look and heavy blow!
> Show more of sacred daring! . . . .
> Lift your torches higher!
> In men's souls ye kindle fire;
> Err—but dare!
> The chains of ages will pass,
> Only that which is taken by force
> Will live, and will be sacred,
> Will be sacred forever! . . . .
> *—Tarassov.*

We are now ready, perhaps, to understand the workingmen's spirit of revolt. Their indignation against the industrial slavery of the old régime gives us the key. Their cries and their exclamations are a physical relief, an easy breathing after years of oppression. No wonder that the revolution appeared to the workers in the image of a "radiant and beloved one." "Great she was," they thought, for she told them that "the long night's death-like sleep is over," that they were no longer "slaves," but "legions" who

> Have come to trample Yesterday
> Under boots shod with anger . . . .
> We have summoned death for a moment,
> To burn the putrid past. . . . .
> *—Alexandrovsky.*

"Soaring like a whirlwind to the heavens," the revolution has awakened and aroused the workers to "err—but dare." Their poems—the direct offspring of a tumultuous historic event—become more and more militant. They call to a "dreadful, bloody fight" and not to the legal methods of strife. These are only intolerable relics of the "putrid past."

Marxism has been the peculiar master force of the
Russian workingmen. The social ideas of Marx and Engels
have shaped the course of their thought and imagination
during many years. The principles of the unfathomed
might of the city proletariat, of its supremacy, of the
sacredness of the class struggle, became supreme among
the workers. And the influence of these conceptions on
their poetry is apparent. We have hardly a poem, whatever its subject, not thrilled through and through by the
consciousness of class struggle.

> In the storms the wires ring
> Of terrible confusion.
> For the black host there is no salvation
> From the workmen's revolution;
> For the black host there is no salvation,
> And never will there be!
>
> Not for a prayer have we come;
> We have left our murky dens
> For a dreadful, bloody fight. . . . .
> —*Berdnikov.*
>
> A winged hurricane we have awakened,
> And with shells we have ploughed the fields:
> We demand full payment
> For the centuries, killed by sleep.
> —*Alexandrovsky.*

Bolder and bolder become their songs, stronger and
stronger grows their hatred for "the black host." The
intensity of their verses springs from the intensity of their
mood. They let themselves be carried away by their excitement and intensify it to the utmost. In their exultation
they become cruel and demand "full payment for the cen-

turies killed by sleep.'' The spirit of revolt whispers evil thoughts in their restless hearts. They grow brutal and rough and assail with railing and scorn all the other classes of Russian society. Since they, now the strongest, have arrived at the top, and all the others, now the weakest, have been forced to the depths, ''there will be no salvation for the black hosts,'' the *bourgeoisie*. And nothing that excites and agitates men against the *bourgeois* class is ever abjured. Their goal, they say, can be reached only through a complete breaking down of all tradition, through the fury of a deadly fight with all the past. And they have come ''to sing a requiem mass'' to the *bourgeoisie* and ''to the past age.''

In their loud and noisy hymns to the ''bright Future,'' the proletarian bards, unlike the peasant poets, completely turned away from the inheritance of the past. The only thing that they now value is the dictatorship of the Proletariat which they never cease to exalt and deify. The knowledge that the city proletariat has become the only ruling class of the country intoxicates them.

> All were drunk, without vodka intoxicated;
> From dawn to dawn all were wide awake. . . . .
> —*Kirillov.*

Convinced that they have already ''thrown down the burden of oppressing inheritance,'' the proletarian singers in their artistic fervor burst through all bonds and restrictions, and launched of a sudden all the pent-up passion of years. In their flush of ecstasy, in their enraptured intoxication they have forgotten that grave and weighty problems are awaiting the working class. The social revolution, passing like "a winged hurricane," has become formidable enough to inspire in everyone solicitous thought. But to the proletarians it is simply a time for agitation and emotion, not for calm and self-poise. Those were "volcanic days," when all the old standards of value collapsed, when all former ideals went down to frightful destruction.

> We sacrilegiously wrecked
> The bounds of ancient laws. . . . .
> —*Ionov.*
> We shall no longer abide
> By the old laws of Adam and Eve,
> The jade of history to death we will drive. . . . .
> —*Mayakovsky.*

Instead of decrying the lust for fighting and annihilation, the proletarian poets encourage it. Those who have had "the courage to challenge society with ideas" now clamor: "Death to the tyrants in the days of freedom" (Berdnikov). And the "tyrants" are not only their former oppressors but all those who fail to agree with them in their visionary views and dogmas.

There is no doubt that the workingmen "trampled yesterday under boots shod with anger." They have not known how to control their passion, how to repress their fiery temperament. They wished to throw off at once all "the burden of oppressing inheritance." The spirit of negation was driven to the last possible limits. Destruction was at work and the end of it could be only chaos. And it was, the chaos of brutal nihilism, of hatred, of lawless and remorseless self-gratification.

CHAPTER IX

COMMUNISM, WORLD REVOLUTION, ATHEISM

We will forge happiness for our native land . . . .
We are force, we are one single will. . . . .
—Semenovsky.
We are all, we are in all, we are the conquering fire and light,
We are to ourselves God, Judge, and Law. . . . .
—Kirillov.
. . . . The path will be cleared soon
For the Brotherhood of the oppressed of all countries and
races. . . . . *—Sadofiev.*

We have seen that the proletarian poets welcomed the
revolution with ecstatic hymns, and that those November
days intoxicated their souls with boundless rapture. We
have noted that their joyful uproar was but the outcry of
men who had too long been kept silent and who, upon
being freed, shouted to the top of their lungs. This wild
and piercing cry of joy celebrated their liberation. Their
hearts yearned ardently for all kinds of sensations. Their
bodies had grown stronger, their souls had become more
cheerful, and their songs were filled with joyous happiness.
Carried away by enthusiasm, they sang the glory of the
long-awaited day.

But to say that the proletarian poets confined themselves to the glorification of the revolution would be to

diminish their stature. For as soon as their first exuberance had died away, they turned their vision toward a new and better social order than that under which they had lived before. In their conception the image of the Russian revolution would be incomplete without their new God, known under the generic name of Communism. They therefore endeavor to shape its form, its organism, and its soul; they glorify it in inspired songs and become the poetic voice of its aims.

The social revolution, coming as it did rather unexpectedly, as a gift fallen from heaven, completely turned the heads of the proletarian poets. In that moment of exultation they imagined that the workingmen were possessors of supernatural strength; that they could at will uproot the social structure not only of Russia, but of the whole world. They also endowed the workers with enormous creative powers and fancied that they would be able to transform the earth into a real Eden. That they

> Without fail will make a golden life,
> The flame, the light of an ideal. . . . .
>
> —*Filipchenko.*

Picturing the proletariat class as a ''New Messiah,'' and continually asserting its superiority over all other classes of society, the bards cry out in ecstasy:

> One more effort of the cradle of the Commune,
> And the Sun of New Life will shine upon the earth. . . . .
>
> —*Sadofiev.*

This is rather generous and enthusiastic anticipation! It is based, however, upon one important thought of these visionary poets, the thought of the unfathomed might of the proletariat class whose "terrible name is the name of Colossus." Indeed nothing but unbounded faith in the all-powerful strength of the working class could have inflamed the minds of the champions of Communism with the presumption that through the Russian "Commune" a "Sun of New Life" would "shine upon the earth." It is true that the communistic idea was then in the very air these poets breathed. And the political life of their country gradually enriched their visions with the suggestions of that idea. They soon recognized its importance for their class and accepted it without hesitation. By a sudden stroke the workingmen became in their own eyes sufficiently strong to reconstruct all Russian life on a basis totally nonexistent as yet in any human society. And in order to uplift the spirit of all the proletarians they began to sing their new idea in exulting, noisy songs, to paint it in the reddest colors, so that it might be heard and seen everywhere.

Thus infinite enthusiasm for the communistic age and great confidence in the power of their class become henceforth the dominant notes in their poetry.

The proletarian poets, wishing to speak to the crowds and to give expression to the feelings of the masses, have little in common with those who give vent to their own, individual emotions. Most, if not all, of the world's great poets, have been largely personal in their appeal, have depicted their own suffering, and have sung their own private griefs. In all great poetry, except perhaps in that which celebrates revenge and war, the individualistic element prevails. But in the proletarian muse there is almost no sign of it. She is inspired by a different passion. Proletarian poetry does not express the poet's personal yearnings, but the longings and emotions of the whole working class. And so, in contrast to the individualistic traits of the prerevolutionary Russian poets, who shut up the world in their own "I," the proletarian bards surrender their ego to the collective "We." For their poetic aim is not to analyze themselves to themselves, not to express their personal cravings, but to analyze themselves as parts of "Labor's countless legions." It must be that long years of suffering in common, of hoping in common, have welded them into one collective soul, into an indissoluble unity. At any rate, their poems show that they all feel socially, and are all subject to the power of collectivism.

> The thought and will of the Collective
> Are our guides. . . . .
>
> —*Loginov.*
>
> In the communistic faith
> We believe collectively. . . . .
>
> —*Kuznetsov.*

Everyone of them constantly speaks in the name of the whole proletariat class and almost every poem begins with a majestic "We."

> We are free like the wind in the field,
> In bondage we will never be;
> Aflame are the wires of steel
> With the fire of our great will.

We are passion, we are power, we are motion,
We are an impulse, we are a boisterous thought . . . .
Over all, and without exception
Reigns the mighty and terrible ''Collective.''
                                        —*Arsky.*

We are the factory's peal and drone,
The smile of young and bright dawns.
We are the fire-faced rays of the rising sun
Of revolutionary days—joyful, crimson.

We are daring. There is no limit to us,
We pierce with our sight mute space. . . . .

We are the embodiment of the coarsely-clad masses,
The seditious blood cells in people's veins;
We are omnipotent, boundless;
We sing the song for the new ages.
                                        —*Yurin.*

They all cling to the concept of the collective ''We.''
This concept is the underlying principle, the foundation,
the firm basis upon which stands their whole communistic
structure. The gist of their idea is that since all Russian
workingmen believe ''collectively'' in the communistic
faith;'' since they all have a boundless admiration for the
''mighty Collective''; since they are united into ''one
single will,'' nothing is unattainable for them. Into this
conception of the united spirit and will of their class, the
proletarian poets put all the fancies that satisfy their
imagination. Trusting that they are ''omnipotent,'' that
they possess ''a creative mind,'' that there is no limit to
their daring, they fancy that they can destroy the whole
old world and erect in its place a ''workingman's palace,''
a ''solar building.''

> We'll blow up and destroy everything.
> We'll wipe everything from the face of the earth.
> We'll extinguish the old sun;
> We'll light up a new sun!
> O'er the old abyss of the world
> We'll build strong bridges;
> We'll erect a solar building
> Of love, rectitude, and beauty. . . . .
>
> —*Arsky.*

It is obvious that the presumptuous idea that the workingman can accomplish anything he wishes is drawn from over-confidence in the powers of the collective "We." And the naïveté, the boastfulness, and oratorical eloquence of the proletarian bards are due to their scanty culture, to their ignorance. They do not seem to know that the greatest thinkers of the world have for centuries been stumbling over the insoluble problem of how to erect "a solar building of love, rectitude, and beauty." They do not comprehend that brute force and fearlessness will not suffice to light up "a new sun." To believe that in following the materialistic conceptions of Marx and Engels the working class will be able to bring to the world "light and revelation from the depths of ages," is ludicrous and absurd. Self-conceit alone could make the proletarian bards obstinately shout:

> We, full of pride, build; we, full of pride, build:
> We build the workmen's palace. . . . .
>
> —*Pomorsky.*
>
> Our workingmen's thought burns
> With the knowledge of labor,
> We—the great architects, the creators,
> Fear no disasters . . . .

> In our hearts is no indecision;
> Our gave is clear, so is our reason. . . . .
> *—Smirnov-Simbirsky.*

In the strength of the belief that the working masses are omnipotent and omniscient the optimistic bards hand over all authority to them. Because the masses alone can "forge happiness for their native land," there is no need to consult the other classes of Russian society. In fact all these may even be immolated, for,

> He who is not a blacksmith is not a man. . . . .
> *—Filipchenko.*

And because only workers are men, they alone should be at the helm of state, even though the majority of the Russian people be against it. The proletariat can rule without their approval and following. Its own will must be the supreme law, its own power must prevail. Besides, the social order of the old world will be all the more readily and easily vanquished if the workingmen are masters. "Happiness for future ages" will never be achieved through the "*bourgeois* class." Only the masses can sweep away all the world's ills and evils and create "a paradise."

> The masses are the forges,
> The masses are the furnaces, foundries;
> Convulsively, persistently working,
> Their paradise they are incessantly creating. . . . .
>
> The masses are forging,
> The masses persistently smite,
> They shape from the granite,
> They mould from steel and gold,
> To the muffled sound of the red tocsin—
> O, be praised—happiness for future ages.

The masses forge for themselves an eagle's fate,
They mould themselves in the crucible of the age
Into one superman;
They wish to be and they will become one titanic heart
and mind. . . . .
                                                    —*Filipchenko.*

These are the thoughts that perpetually recur in the poems of the proletarians. In their materialistic ideology of life the working masses become the guiding spirit, the symbol of wisdom and justice for the new age. The "masses" are "the crown of creation" and the "levers of the universe." They alone are mature enough to "stand like a firm wall" against old superstitions, against every kind of oppression, against all "the camarilla of masters." The "masses" will subdue to their will "fire, water, iron stone"; they will "enchant all living with the same passion"; they will reign over all, and proclaim themselves "God, Judge and Law."

The protagonists of communism do not realize that they have taken too heavy a burden upon their shoulders. Only arrogant self-assurance and obstinate vanity could inspire this faith that the Russian proletariat is wise and just in its aims and purposes. They certainly judge from their own brains and their own experience. But one cannot help thinking that their judgments are erroneous. For if the Russian proletariat class were really so high-minded and so idealistic as its poets picture it; if its reason were really clear, how then could one account for its extreme injustice toward all those Russians who have struggled to raise their country intellectually and spiritually? It cannot be denied that the proletariat's attitude toward many

Russians who sacrificed their lives for art, science, and political liberty has been far from wise and righteous. It is not an exaggeration to say that the high virtues ascribed to the Russian proletariat exist only in the imagination of its bards.

The ideas and expectations of the proletarian poets may seem visionary to us, but not so to them. They "know all" and their "gaze is clear." Their zealous faith in communism is so great that they have no doubts about anything. They even accept as an indubitable truth what to many seems an indubitable error, that in destroying everything old they are carrying a new message to the world.

> Destroying all barriers
> And all obstacles,
> We march forward,
> Bringing a new revelation
> To the universe. . . . .
> *—Sadofiev.*

This "new revelation" that they are "bringing to the universe" is international communism. The wide vision of world revolution kindles their spirit and feeds the flame of their artistic passion. Their craving is now to transplant the Russian "Eden" to all foreign lands.

> Hear ye! Journeymen of the world's plantations,
> Factories, fields, quarries,
> Blue-bloused men of all races and nations:
> Destroy all strawlike weakness! . . . .
> *—Obradovich.*

Since 1918 they have been hoping and expecting that the proletariat of the world would rise. Lenin himself

had told them, immediately after the peace treaty of Brest
Litvosk, that the humiliation and burdens which the Cen-
tral Powers were placing upon the Russian people were a
matter of indifference, because the Russian revolution was
the starting point of the world revolution.

> The masses . . . . closely encircle the tribune,
> Proclaiming Brotherhood, the Commune,
> As their indissoluble, reciprocal union;
> And, with the ringing tocsin,
> The summoning brass, they celebrate;
> Turbulently, joyfully they await
> Lenin, dearer to them than a brother . . . .
> From the tribune he will tell them,
> In the words of the Messiah,
> Of Communism in Soviet Russia
> And of the universal victory of the proletariat. . . . .
>
> —*Malashkin.*

Now since their most revered leader assured them that
"the universal victory of the proletariat" was only a
matter of a few months, there could be no doubt in their
minds that it was coming. Lenin could not be mistaken.
Besides, before Lenin's death, there had already been
some promising attempts made by the proletariat of certain other countries to bring about the communistic era.
It was true that those attempts were not of great magnitude
in comparison with the "universal victory" of the workingmen so confidently expected. Yet they clearly indicated to
the proletarian poets that there was great hope for it, and
they continued to cherish their delusions. But as time
went on and the world revolution did not come to pass, the
bards grew more and more restless. Having realized that

the existence of communism in Russia largely depended on the support of the workers of the world, they felt that they must summon them to their aid. And in inspired words they began to call to their banners "the family of the workers' Commune."

> For the sake of the common fate of our brothers,
> You, the proletarians of all the world,
> With one strong will, one mighty effort
> Rally to your great camp!
> Rush to the rescue of communards,
> Break serfdom's fetters,
> Let the tumultuous tide scatter
> At one sweep the old world. . . . .   —*Ionov.*

Here the proletarian poets went beyond the confines of the Marxian theories, according to which revolutions cannot be artificially made, but must arise spontaneously out of conditions. They completely ignored world conditions and naïvely believed that all the countries were ripe for their highest ideal, for communism. They therefore addressed their appeal to all the workers of the world. Strange as it may seem, it worked like a magic wand. Immediately, though, to be sure, in the imagination of the proletarian poets alone, the "brotherhood of all countries and races" responded to the call, and began to join the Russian communists in their revolt against the former world.

> The pavements, the black throats of the mines,
> The mountains, the earth's crust, the towns
> In America, Africa, Asia, and Europe,
> In the east and west, in the south and north,
> Consumed with maddening fires,
> Groan from dawn to dawn. . . . .   —*Filipchenko.*

. . . . I hear the hymn of Marseillaise
And the distant cadence of steps:
I see the barricades; the countless moving masses;
The corpses of bankers and tsars; the broken fetters!

I see: the distance is red with flames;
'Tis milliards of crimson flags and banners float. . . . .
Under them—triumphant, proud, bold,
Our international Comrade—Proletariat—enters the world.
. . . .

With electricity the thick air is saturated,
And all the countries are a rumbling volcano. . . . .
I feel: the path will be cleared soon
For the brotherhood of the oppressed of all countries and
races. . . . .

—*Sadofiev.*

They are now more exuberant than ever. The world
revolution is no longer in the distant future; it is coming to
them right now, and it will work miracles. In their exalted
mood they all hear its "loud peals resound," and behold
its "dawn aflame."

From our towers we already behold:
Across the sea,
O'er foreign fields and plains
The revolution's dawn is aflame. . . . .
The call is heard beyond the ocean,
The first loud peals resound.
Proud Albion, like a terrible tempest,
May rise at any moment.
We are not alone. . . . . Behold, ye brothers,
The same emblem across the sea:
The sheaf and the hammer, the plough and the sickle
Are interlaced in one single embrace.

—*Ionov.*

So "the revolution's dawn" continues to illumine the days of their "bright future." Millions of workers will struggle on and will hold aloft "the torchlight of red," thus clearing the "path to the brotherhood of the oppressed of all countries and races." In their ecstasy they leap over all barriers and obstacles and earnestly hope that the universe will soon belong to the proletariat class alone. Greater illusions than these are impossible. The lack of understanding of the proletarian poets is both amazing and irritating. Few men can share their dream that international brotherhood will be realized through violent revolutions. The Russian proletarians are victims of Marxian prejudices. For it is not the mad strife of revolution, but the gradual advance of refined culture and enlightenment that will bring about the brotherhood of nations. Whatever the proletarians may say to the contrary, forcible revolution can never lead to any satisfactory solution of human ills, much less to the realization of international brotherhood.

In their optimism these prophets of the world-uprising derive new strength for their activity. Since the union of the workers of the world is but a question of weeks, of days, since it is beyond all doubt that "proud Albion" will rise, they prepare themselves for that moment which must inevitably come. Meanwhile they haughtily and joyfully sing:

We are Labor's countless, unyielding legions,
We have conquered the expanse of seas, of land, and of ocean,
We have illumined towns with the light of artificial sun:
Our proud souls burn with a rebellious fire.

> We love life, and its intoxicating boisterous ecstasy,
> Our spirit is tempered with a terrible struggle and agony.
> We are all, we are in all, we are the conquering fire and light,
> We are to ourselves God, Judge, and Law.
>
> —*Kirillov.*

When one class of society comes out and takes upon itself the right to be "God, Judge, and Law," anarchy and disaster always come to that society. For it usually ignores the will of all other classes, and antagonizes them; and the consequence of this must be revolt and a complete breakdown of the state whose sole arbiter that class has become. It is particularly true that might and justice are hostile to each other. Selfish men are mutually antagonistic. The law in the hands of selfish men who wish "to forge an eagle's fate for themselves," for their class alone, becomes one of the greatest sources of material and spiritual disaster. There have been in recent years many examples of such calamities among the European peoples. The Russian revolution itself is the most signal illustration of this kind of disaster.

Being to themselves "God, Judge, and Law," the proletarian poets firmly believe in one power only, that of the man-god, the man-creator.

> There is no God . . . .
> Man is superior to God,
> Man is the creator of God. . . . .
>
> —*Filipchenko.*

They laugh at existing religions, at morality, and at idealistic philosophy. Their sole and final guide for all their problems and needs is the materialistic philosophy of their teachers, Marx and Engels. In their conception of society, in their emphasis on the class struggle and on the might and the capacities of the proletariat class, in their negation of all religions and in their belief in the man-god, the influence of that philosophy is quite obvious. And they proclaim it superior to all other philosophical systems. They believe with Trotsky that there is more true science in the "Communist Manifesto" alone than in all other historico-philosophical works. Furthermore, the proletarian poets, while studying that true science in order to learn from it the easiest way to create their earthly Eden, have forgotten the Kingdom of Heaven.

> We have forgotten to sigh and yearn for Heaven. . . . .
> *—Kirillov.*

They have also forgotten:

> The prayers and books of Buddha,
> Mohammed, Christ, and others. . . . .
> *—Obradovich.*

The scientific philosophy of the "Communist Manifesto" may alarm every one but the proletarian bards themselves. Them it convinced that the world's wisdom is not to be found in the teachings of Christ, of Buddha, or of Mohammed, but in the workingman's hammer.

> I have learned that all the world's wisdom is in this
> hammer. . . . .   *—Kirillov.*

In their thought the workingman's "hammer" is the world's finest wisdom, and it symbolizes the material life which "the masses are forging" in the factories and foundries. For the paradise that they wish to create is not the ethereal paradise of religious teachings, but a very material and tangible one. And to their mind it is the communistic paradise that will bring happiness to Russia and to the rest of the world.

It is apparent that religion is not the guiding spirit in the philosophy of the proletarian poets. In their conception religion is the greatest evil, "opium for the people," and therefore harmful to the future ideal society. Interpreting history and all the phenomena of the universe from the purely materialistic point of view, they come to the conclusion that religion is an anachronism, an outlived factor, not needed by "minds enlightened by combats." To them the economic factor alone is the basis of society. They believe that it is only necessary to change society's economic structure, and all the other factors of life, spiritual as well as political, will then change of their own accord. They further claim that the proletariat class has already attained enough wisdom, enough intelligent sense of self-protection, to become the only "Master of the world." It therefore does not need the trivial stimulation coming from worship and prayer: it wishes to listen only to "stormy songs" and to "spasmodic groans."

In denying that the spiritual element is an important factor in the development of society, the communistic philosophy of the proletarian poets becomes shallow and superficial enough. Being reduced to pure materialism, it loses the depth and profundity of a more conscious approach to human problems, and renders its disciples

indifferent to the deep understanding of the subtle under-
currents of all life.

The principles of communism and atheism have brought
the proletarian bards to the belief that they are "life's
reason" and the "world's genius." Because they alone
are the carriers of that light and truth which will bring
harmony and beauty of the universe, they identify themselves with the greatest geniuses of the world.

> To proud daring there is no limit,
> We are Wagner, Leonardo, Titian.
> On the new museum we shall build
> A cupola like that of Montblanc.
>
> In the crystal marbles of Angelo,
> In all the wonder of Parnassus,
> Is there not the song of creative genius
> That like an electric current throbs in us?
>
> We laid the stones of the Parthenon,
> And those of the giant Pyramids;
> Of all the Sphinxes, temples, Pantheons
> We have cut the clanging granite.
>
> Was it not for us that on Mount Sinai,
> In the burning bush,
> The red Banner glowed, like the sun
> Amidst storm and fire?
>
> We shall take all, we shall know all,
> We shall pierce the turquoise of the skies;
> We shall pierce the depths to the bottom. . . . . .
>
> —*Gerasimov.*

This boasting self-conceit and self-gratification is inspired by the state of ecstasy which springs from the faith
of being men-gods, men-creators. But it again shows that

the proletarian poets overestimate the extent of the workingmen's strength and capabilities. When affirming that
they will "know all," that they will "embrace all the
boundless mystery," they do not seem to realize at all the
scope of human powers in general. Real thinkers who
have already come in contact with the search for "all"
know the confines of truth and are conscious of the impos-
sibility of piercing "the depths to the bottom."

Too hastily have the proletarian singers ascribed to
themselves the honor of being "Wagner, Leonardo, and
Titian." Centuries of creative thought and art have
brought humanity to those highest peaks, and our new
poets crown themselves too soon with such laurels. While
it is true that they are "Labor's countless, rigorous
legions," they have not as yet created "a cupola like
Montblanc." Poverty of thought alone can account for
the identification of their own destructive spirit with great
creative minds. For hitherto they have possessed only the
force to destroy, to negate, to tread down all the past,
and to express a desire for a better future. They have not
yet brought to the world any "new light," any "new
sun." It may be that in the course of the horrible destruction of their country, they have taken the blazing fires of
the old cupolas for the light of their "new sun."

CHAPTER X

"THE IRON MESSIAH"

The factory rose on the earth,
Triumpant and bright, like the sun. . . . .
> —*Obradovich.*

There are calls in iron
Full of tingling ire;
With the clamor of metal
Something stirs and rises,
Something sparkles in the depth of eyes. . . . .
> —*Gerassimov.*

The proletarian singers, sons of the social revolution and true exponents of its aims, find genuine inspiration in things and places where earlier Russian poets had discovered no stimulus. The factory and the machine, iron and steel, never attracted the poets of prerevolutionary Russia. They regarded them as monsters crushing the human soul, as crude and ugly objects unworthy of poetic treatment. The Russian prose writers when speaking of the factory used to represent it as a symbol of slavery, and the machines as an evil force annihilating the free will of the individual. The great Tolstoy, for instance, strongly condemned factories and industrialism. He pointed to primitive man, who produced all his necessities from his own resources, with his own hands independent of any factory, of any machine.   Moreover, the laborers themselves were always hostile to the factory, and considered everything connected with it as "the Lord's curse."

> O seditious, fiery, passionate factory,
> O, thou who hast reared me!
> For many years thou didst stoop my back. . . . .
>
> . . . .
>
> Crucified upon thine iron bars,
> I cursed "the city-octopus"
> And the wicked, servile labor,
> By eternal serfdom branded . . . .
> To the son of pines and heather
> Thine iron embraces
> Were the Lord's curses
> And the devil's powerful fetters. . . . .
>
> *—Sadofiev.*

But the social revolution has changed all standards of value; yesterday's conceptions are no longer those of today. What seemed to their predecessors, and even to their fellow-workers, injurious, baneful, and ugly, now appears to the proletarian poets beneficial, healthy and beautiful. Factories and machines, iron and steel, become to them at once the powerful instruments, the titanic forces, that will help the proletarian class to "crush the yoke of destiny" and "conquer the enchanting world." For such a state of mind there naturally can be no hostility to the factory, furnace, forge, and lathe. Indeed, these are now the center of their hearts and of their poems. They forcefully sing their usefulness, their power, their beauty, and through every line of their songs throbs a passion for them, unknown to all former Russian poets.

The factory leads to the red carnival,
Through its fiery gates,
Those who in the Commune do not believe,
Who prayed for our peril!
There, happiness will last forever,
And the factory—turbulent, ardent—
With the galaxy of its cupolas
Will kindle the flame of the Future.

And the lifeless hand
Will never still
The moving factory fly-wheel,
Christened in the bloody stream. . . . .

                              Sadofiev.

The factory is mighty, menacing, drunken . . . .
It flares with a bright red
Surpassing the sunset of crimson . . . .
It looks proudly at the azure heavens.

It scatters shiny coins
Of sparks that laugh with thunder,
And the sun turns pale before it . . . .
Stately is the giant of steel.

There it is—the stern and bold knight—
It has thrown up the shaggy smoke,
Sooty, its face like fire;
It blusters with a muffled roar.

Forward it stares with a gaze of fire
Into the dark night.
Its martial armor is its pride . . . .
With passionate breath it sings. . . . .

                              —Tikhomirov.

And it sings to them of the might of technical science
which, in conquering the elemental forces of nature, will
hand over the mastery of the world to their class. All the

proletarian poets look reverently upon the power of science. They earnestly believe that this power alone will relieve the workers from the drudgery of strenuous labor, and will afford them possibilities of rising into higher realms of life, thought, beauty, and vision. Therefore they prostrate themselves before the "Iron Messiah," "the lord of the earth," from whom they await their salvation and their social independence.

> There he is—the Savior, the lord of the earth,
> The ruler of titanic forces—
> In the roar of countless steel machinery,
> In the sparkle of suns of electricity.
>
> . . . .
>
> To the world he brings the New Sun,
> He destroys the thrones and prisons:
> He calls the peoples to eternal fraternity,
> And wipes out the boundary lines.
>
> His crimson banner—the symbol of struggle
> For the oppressed—is the guiding beacon;
> With it we shall crush the yoke of destiny,
> We shall conquer the enchanting world.
>
> —*Kirillov.*

The factory thus becomes to the workers one of the most important agents of their salvation. It is no longer a cursed slavery enchaining human beings and killing their initiative, their creative force, their mind and body. It now appears as "the Saviour," as the destroyer of "thrones and prisons," as the guiding spirit of the oppressed in their fight for freedom. In their boundless love for the "Iron Messiah" they visualize the factory as the only revelation, as the only bright spark of hope for a future happier life—on this earth, be it understood, not beyond the grave. And amidst the incessant clamor of the machines they hear a new symphony which is to them infinitely more powerful and melodious than that of nature. It stirs their souls to the depths and arouses new emotions in their hearts.

> Only today I have felt, only today I have learned,
> Here, in the factory, the daily, noisy, festive carnival.
> The peals and cadence of ringing uproar—the speech of sounds without words,
> The shapely rhythmical dance of sheaves, joyful and drunken.
> In the dance there is the dream of youth, eternal motion, and freedom.
> In the sounds, the world's secret, in the sounds, the world's wisdom,
> In the songs, vigor, inspiration, burning faith, challenge and anger.
> Oh, how sweet it is to hear this tune so passionately ardent,
> . . . .
> To understand the iron tongue, to hear the mystery of a revelation;
> To be in the factory daily, to be there, is ecstasy!
> —*Sadofiev.*

Everything connected with the factory inspires the proletarian muse with ecstasy. The huge machines that had in old times repelled many a workingman now lure them all as poetic symbols of "the mystery of revelation." Even the factory whistles, feared formerly as the messengers of despair and submission, are now hailed and welcomed as heralds of hope and triumph.

> There is nothing more appealing, masterful,
> Clear, ardent, and tuneful,
> More inspiring and beautiful,

And triumphant and free,
Than the early morning prayer of the fused and tuneful chorus
Of the factory whistles, calling to fight, startling the night.

. . . .

Trembling, and listening to the song,
I comprehend the wisdom of the world:
The choir of whistles—the universal tongue,
The hymn of unity, the hymn of Labor,
The awakening of the imprisoned thought,
The wires from heart to heart.
To the Man-God rises this song, to the Victor, the Fighter,
To the indefatigable Creator, to the Titan Artist. . . . .

—Sadófiev.

The "multifaced creators," the workingmen in the
suburbs and the cities, listen to the tuneful chorus of the
whistles as to a morning prayer. And while "trembling"
and "listening" to this tune, they imagine that they comprehend the "wisdom of the world." Then with proud
hearts they joyfully go forth to the factories, where they
"incessantly create something all new and different." The
whistles now sing to them the finest melody, the "hymn of
unity," of "Labor," of "awakening thought" that sends
"wires from heart to heart" of the workers. And filled
with ecstasy, they themselves begin to sing with fervor:

Great eternal Labor! To thee be the praise!
With thy dew didst thou bathe us in the foundry's furnace,
With a masterly hand didst thou weld into a single rhythm
The slow beat of hearts and the rumble of anvils.

—Ionov.

The factory whistles become the symbol of the great
awakening of the mind of the proletariat. And they suggest to the workers that "Man," in subjugating to his

needs the machines, steel and iron, will become "God," the only "Creator," the only "Titan-Artist."

The factories which "have risen on the earth triumphant and bright, like the sun," will be "the animating temples of the soul," the modern cathedrals and palaces of the workers. These enormous "temples" seem to the proletarian poets miraculously beautiful, for they are not relics of the past, but predict to them their future communistic reign. It is only there that they kneel and pray, and in the fantastic liturgy played by the music of the machines that "peal, roar, dance, and sing," they hear ecstatic hymns which give them wings to rise "to the skies," to the highest spheres of human emotion.

A striking characteristic of the spirit of the proletarians, of the strife of their soul, and of their fixed conviction of the final conquest of the factory and the machine, is beautifully portrayed in Sadofiev's poem "At the Lathe."

> . . . . With the dance of wheels .
> Two desires in my bosom, two great principles dispute. . . . .
> In the soft murmur of the belts a voice I hear:
> "O poet, free-thinker, dreamer!
> Wert thou born into this world
> To suffer torments in the factory all thy life,
> That chained to the machines thou shouldst die?

And the factory begins to appear to him sordid, dark, a horrible place that dims his eyes with filth and gloom. From the babble and boom of the monster machines his mind becomes dull, his back aches; his body, his soul, and his free individual will are annihilated. All his inner being resents this entire subjugation to the machine. It

craves and yearns to be in the open, to gaze at the blue sky,
to feel the warmth of the sun, to breathe the invigorating
air of mountains and seas, and to listen to the caressing
tunes of nature. The same voice tells him that:

> There is spring outside your window . . . . beauty . . . . glit-
> tering sun . . . .
> There—a chorus of feathery songsters caresses the ear,
> Over there is the fragrance of the flowers, the trees.
> And see how kindly the sun looks,
> How tenderly he kisses, how much joy he pours forth;
> He teases, lures, and calls persistently
> To the open boundless plains, to freedom,
> To the green and flowery carpet . . . .
> To the resounding sea and the playful surf,
> To the mountains! Higher . . . .
> Nearer to the sun! To the skies! . . . .

Enchanted by these words and craving for happiness
and joy, the worker at the lathe begins to curse the factory's prison and decides to flee "toward the sun, the sea,
the hills, toward freedom." But here the other voice in-
sistently breaks in, no less powerful and convincing. It
launches a mighty protest against the atavistic instincts
of the past, when the city worker was still a peasant, a
slave of the elements, of his landlord, and of every kind
of superstition. This "steely voice" cries out:

> Curse not the factory, the lathes and the machines!
> Hither you came from the sunny vale,
> Where—under the henchman's yoke—you were a slave
> Here you curse the metal that calls to fight,
> There you groaned under your master's whip . . . .
> Here the belts talk to you of the sun;
> When you suffered there, you were not glad to see the
> light. . . . .
> . . . .

There—under a cart you slept in the fields;
There—you wandered humble and lonely:
Here—the factory has united you all in one!
There—you pined in long and dreadful anguish,
Here—the talk, the heat of the machines calls you to free-
    dom! . . . .
There—the priest dazed you with a false creed,
Here—the factory has set your reason free:
It pours into your breast vigor, faith, protest, wrath.
And leads you out upon the pure and fiery road!
Here—the meaning of Life, the aim of Life is made clear to
    you . . . .
Here is the fount of all striving and revolt!

So the worker, now quite convinced that this voice has
told him the truth, remains at the lathe. The factory is
no longer a curse, but a blessing. It radiates a light of
uncommon beauty, and guides him to the highest wisdom.
The babble and boom of the machines now turn into a soft
melody that arouses happy dreams of a bright future. The
voice now entreats him to listen intently to the talk of the
machines. For it tells the worker that he will dominate
all life and be the one ruling force of the universe:

Only listen and understand the talk of the machines:
You—the future Master, you—the Messiah . . . .
With steam, steel, and fire you are allied.
You will capture the globe. . . . .

So in agony and perplexity the worker has heard the
"two great principles" dispute in his bosom. The joyous
enthusiasm with which the first voice filled his soul has
soon passed away. It has been succeeded by an ardent
faith in the other voice, whose reasoning has proved strong
enough to destroy forever all the atavistic remnants in his

soul. Having fathomed the mysteries of the past and of the "Iron Messiah," the worker throws aside the first and greets the coming reign of the second.

> Burying in tombs the Past,
> The Soviet citizen can see
> In this cosmic avalanche
> The factory's creative force.
> In thy triumphant rumble
> The prayers and psalms are drowned . . . .
> Not to believe in miracles hast thou taught us,
> But to create happiness upon this earth. . . . .
> —*Sadofiev.*

Having drunk deep in the atmosphere of the factory, whence proceed "vigor, faith, protest, wrath," the worker can no longer "believe in the miracles of the past." It is the factory that now becomes his "soul's mistress," the "fount of all his strivings," all the wisdom of the world, which he tries to understand, to know and to celebrate in loving song.

> O, thou elemental force, my soul's mistress,
> The lightning arrow of my thought!
> To thee I sing my sounding song—
> For thee is my ardent heart's blood.
>
> . . . .
>
> To me thou art still dearer now,
> Still more longed for, my own!
> I swear by the love of our youth,
> By the joy of the days of the future;
>
> I shall not cease to kiss thee,
> My mistress and mother,
> Dynamo—Industry!
> I shall not cease to sing to thee,
> My mistress and mother
> This melodious liturgy!   —*Sadofiev.*

The factory is to the proletarian poets the final, absolute good. It is their "mistress and mother," the "lightning arrow" of their thoughts. In its "triumphant rumble" they feel a strong and mighty power, an "elemental force" which enraptures and uplifts their souls. In it "are drowned" their old "prayers and psalms," and beyond it nothing attracts them. Since the factory alone teaches them to create happiness on earth, their love for it becomes so great that they cannot part with it. It is not the light of sky and water, nor the warm rays of the sun, nor the blossoming fields that lure the proletarian poets. The holy mystery of the natural world was revealed to the peasant poets, but not to them. They are inspired by the factory alone, and find great imaginative expression in the vibrating sounds of metal. Away from the factories and the machines, they feel sad and lost. Only when they hear the buzzing of the lathes and the beat of the hammers do they regain their cheerfulness, their strength, and grow more and more active.

> With the ceaselessly buzzing lathes
> I sing the turbulent rhyme;
> Under the blows of steel hammers
> The golden strings sing and whine.
>
> My bosom is full of passionate desires,
> I hear music in the intoxicated tumult.
> The wave of ringing sounds rises,
> And like the wind in the plains, thought flies. . . . .
> —*Tikhomirov.*
>
> In the smithies—red,
> And like Vesuvius menacing,
> In the glitter of turquoise lightning,

> We forge without rest,
> And a sonorous song we sing. . . . .
>
> . . . .
>
> We stamp and grind,
> And ceaselessly gild and light
> The darkness of night. . . . .
>
> . . . .
>
> We forge with joy and cheer,
> And golden gems we scatter,
> To work we summon ever;
> We are lords, we are Titans
> Over fire and iron. . . . .
>
> —*Arsky.*

> Our muscles are strong,
> The muscles of the united workmen's throng,
> Of workmen's metal-like, creative hands,
> Of the world's democracy—a body like a buffalo, and a spirit
>   like a god. . . . .
>
> —*Filipchenko.*

Face to face with the factory and the machines, their imagination, as we see, is possessed by a whirling motion. They ceaselessly "stamp, grind, forge" and "scatter golden gems."

To the proletarian poets iron and steel are not crude and ugly objects that require great effort and patient endeavor to handle. On the contrary, they are light, flexible, and easy to forge and mold. These metals become their nearest and best friends. Looking upon them with loving eyes, they see in them charming and beautiful qualities.

> There is tenderness in iron,
> The frolicking of snowflakes;
> And love glitters, when it is polished;

There is the crimson of sunset,
There are impulse and weariness,
And blood is on the rusty cleft.

There is passion in iron,
There are the turbulence and cadence
Of the waves splashing against rocks:
The siren's melody
In the seething foam,
Where the sinuous body is free.

There is autumn in iron,
The cold blueness
Amidst the rusty pine twigs;
There is the scorching summer heat
Clad in a mirage
Of the fervent, flowering spring.
There is purity in iron. . . . .

. . . .

There are trills of flutes
Which flash and vanish
In the smiles of exultant faces. . . . .

—Gerassimov.

Iron is thus endowed with human emotions. This hard metal becomes sensitive, tender, pure, and passionate. It even reflects the seasons of the year, and its melodious sounds suggest to the poets delightful and captivating images. But above all, it possesses that might from which "giants are reared." They therefore "unite with metal," let their "souls melt in steel," and from this union they feel a great creative strength. They become "Lords," "Titans," powerful, unbreakable, like metal itself.

Striking and very modern is the attitude of the proletarian poets towards this "Dynamo—Industry." The factory, the machines, iron and steel, stir their imagination and their feelings to the highest pitch. All of them devote to the "Iron Messiah" many eloquent poems of much charm. In no poetry, not even in that of Verhaeren, can one find such a passion for the factories, such an exultation in iron, such beautiful descriptions of the forms and sounds of machines, as in this proletarian poetry. Few poets have been so well acquainted as the proletarian with the secret springs of the factory and of machinery, with the instincts of workingmen, with the peculiarities of their passion and temperament. All the magnificent pictures in these poems are drawn from their own experience.

> I have overheard these songs of years dear and joyful
> In the roaring tumult of the fire-faced and vast cities.
>
> I have heard these songs of the golden days of the future
> In the factory turmoil, the clang of steel, and the wicked
>   whisper of the belts.
>
> I have looked at my comrade forging the golden steel,
> And I have seen the wonderful face of the sun of the future.
>
> I have learned that . . . .
> The harder the hammer may beat, break, forge,
> The brighter will joy glitter in the gloomy world.
>
> The swifter the trundles may turn,
> The more alluring and bright will our days shine.
>
> These songs were sung to me by the voices of millions,
> Millions of blue-bloused blacksmiths—brave and strong. . . . .
>
> —*Kirillov.*

To the proletarian poets the factory is not only beautiful in its appearance, but also, and particularly so, in its aims. All their poems dealing with it breathe an air of joyful hope that the factory will bring them their final salvation, therefore they have much affection and love for it. In their souls "full of passionate desires" they feel that "the foundries, like volcanoes, burn up the gray sorrow and woes," therefore they exult in "turbulent songs." In daily contact with technical science, they have learned its strength and its force. The factory has become their god, their "Messiah"; and their religious faith in it speaks eloquently through their verse.

CHAPTER XI

THE PROLETARIAN HYMN TO THE CITY

Upon the factory whistles' solemn call,
With a breath of spring I come
Into the gardens of granite and metal,
Into the avenues of buildings of stone.

I am a stranger to the vagabond wind,
I have forgotten the boundless fields,
The wilderness of native plains,
The soft earth—flowery and green.

The silks of lulling meadows
I gave up for the hard stone,
I love the colorful sparks,
And the street's riotous tumult.

Drifting in the swift stream,
I am a stranger to my soul.
The native fields, the days of old
Have now become a distant dream.

—Gerassimov.

The industrious city, with its countless dwellings and
workshops, with its heavy toil, with its nervous tension
and trembling activity, has become, since the revolution,
one of the most beloved themes of the proletarian muse.
Unlike the peasant poets who, as we have already seen, are
listening solely to the voice of the quiet, peaceful village,

and are passionately singing the harmonious beauty of the
country, the proletarian bards are turning all their affection to the tumultuous and roaring city. They seem to be
constantly attracted by the city's "cries like groans," by
the strange noisy music of its steady vibration, of its rest-
lessness and nervous sensitiveness.

> The city has pulled the smoky crown
> Over the edges of factory stacks;
> It utters cries like groans,
> Gleaming with the steel of its black mouth.
>
> Like the birds of a scattered flock,
> The swift street cars flash.
> In its blazing inferno
> They dart thunderbolts upward.
>
> In the abysses of endless streets
> There swarms the droning human hive.
> There is noise everywhere, the everlasting roar
> Of Labor's mighty life. . . . .
>
> *—Gutsevich.*

The modern city evoked the loathing, hatred, and hostility of almost all the prerevolutionary Russian writers.
To Gogol and Dostoevsky, as well as to Tolstoy and Chekhov, the steel-gray sky and the cloudy smoke of the big
cities were frightful and repulsive. To Andreyev and
Gorky, the two most influential and representative writers
of the period immediately preceding the revolution, the
city appeared as a beast in its passion and as a monster
in its strength. This feeling was emphasized by the most
outstanding poets of the close of the nineteenth and the
beginning of the twentieth centuries. Sologub, Blok, Bely,

and Ivanov could find no new motive, no new shade of color in the sooty breath and in the vast agglomerations of the industrial centers. Under the spell of their own intellectual theories and their own mystical philosophy, these poets seemed to have overheard the singing of the celestial spheres, and to have seen their beauty. In mystic rapture they circled round the eternal azure of heaven, and their eyes were fixed not on reality but on that which soars above. Possessed only by "ideal beauty," they could discover in the cities of iron and concrete, of huge factories and dismal shops, neither external nor inner form, not to speak of beauty. The very aspect of the modern Babylons was repulsive to them. So, like the prose writers, these poets abhorred the city and assumed a hostile attitude to it.

But with the proletarian poets the traditional outlook on the city is changed. Men who have been living for years in dingy and murky streets, who have been deprived of the comforts and luxury of modern life, men who have been shut off from the rays of the sun and from all longing for philosophical ideals, have a radically different conception of the city. They contemplate it with feelings that are bound up with their own life, their own energy, and they are impressed by its power and its utility. The city had repelled their predecessors because they still regarded it with the eyes of the past century, when iron frameworks, machines, locomotives, telephone and telegraph poles were despised, and when industrialism was regarded as a phase of degeneration. Such being their state of mind the pre-revolutionary writers could discover in the city nothing

but unseemliness and ugliness. But to the proletarian
poets, sons of the industrial age and adherents of the cult
of materialistic science, the city, like the factory, displays
as much beauty as the country and as the cathedrals and
palaces of earlier days. It has fair forms, it is well pro-
portioned, it is beautiful in its appearance, and particularly
in its aims.

> Stirring with the new life's riot,
> Clad in emerald and steel,
> There stands, enigmatically austere,
> My city, an octopus, a giant.
>
> . . . .
>
> It is the city of ardent desires!
> It is the heart of the country!
> In it mass revolutions whirl
> And kindle bloody fires.
>
> It is the mighty city, the city-Master,
> It is the guiding star.
> It unfurls the blood-red banner
> Of Labor set free.
>
> *—Gutsevich.*

Thus contemplating the city with love and pleasure, they
extol its magnificence, and celebrate it as the purest form
of "the new source of life." For they feel that an enormous energy emanates from the city, that it is becoming
more and more the center of force, of impulse, and of striving. And since the Russian workingmen of today are
themselves over-heated with effort and struggle, since the
city is "the heart of the country," of "ardent desires"
and of mass revolutions, that is to say of multiplied energy,
there is no wonder that it is to them full of beauty. It is

no longer a "wicked despot," nor a monster with "eyes afire," nor a "sleepless dragon of iron and steel," but the "guiding star" and the "future flowery Eden" of the proletariat.

> O great Red Wizard,
> My wicked despot of yesterday!
> To sing of you I am destined . . . .
> You are the future flowery Eden.
>
> I cannot but love you,
> I shall never forsake you, never;
> To me you are dearer than the flowers of the meadow,
> Than the green grassy plain.
>
> In the limitless starry space,
> Milliards of steel chariots will rumble,
> And you will breathe the life of iron
> Upon the distant planets' wastes.
>
> *—Berdnikov.*

It is very characteristic of the proletarian poets' temperament that the placid and calm country with its magic scenery appeals to them less than the squalor and din of the restless city. Enchanted by the idea of its strength and of the material and intellectual advantages that they can obtain from it, they regard the city as "dearer than the flowers of the meadow, than the green grassy plain." Even those of the proletarian poets who have come from the country to the industrial centers are equally enthralled by the city and its life.

> In childhood days I loved Nature
> With all the ardor of my heart,
> But now—I am the factory's friend;
> Country life has no more lure for me,

Nor the beautiful river bank.
I gave up my rustic home
For the factory whistles in town.
I left for ever
My wide native plains;
To the city with no regret I came,
For it I abandoned my fields;
They could not give me aid,
They yielded naught but want.
In the city there is action and zeal
And life rushes onward.

—*Loginov.*

The reverence of these poets for the great cities has something to do with the new spirit ushered in by the revolution. Indeed, since 1917, the country has become to all city workers the symbol of the past, of staunch conservatism. Nothing good has come from the "plains," the "shabby hamlets," and the "tottering huts." Country life, full of charm and beauty to the peasant poets, looks too dull, too calm, and too stagnant to the proletarians.

You will perish,
You will die,
Ere the Red Cock of the Revolution
Crows thrice.
O village,
Over your corpse
I shall not weep;
My heart will feel no pang.
In the flames of a stormy uprising,
Other things than this have I seen.
Amidst the flames of a stormy uprising
Different flowers grow.
But here—
A cart in summer,

And a sleigh in winter,
Like turtles crawl
Across the fields.
The bast-shoemakers and weavers
Are enmeshed here
From head to toe
With the thick weeds
Of a stupid creed.

I love the city,
The metal and steel
And the granite.
I long to see
Amidst the lacy wilderness of woods,
Upon the flooded meadows,
The live forest of factories
And thousands of the city suns.
                              —Doronin.

To these poets the city alone symbolizes action and progress. Thus they are fascinated and lured by its feverish
whirl, which they hail as the dawn of a new life.

Farther, farther away from the plains,
From the shabby hamlets,
From the tottering huts,
And from pain—
There runs a single road:
Ever toward the city-giant.
Action and struggle
Are possible only in the city.
There is no hope for the plains;
Such is their destiny.
Farther, farther away from the plains,
Into the kingdom of factories and machines,
Into the noisy, vigorous city,
Where the new source of life begins!
                              Loginov.

Now since it is only there that "action and struggle are possible," since the city does not scatter but concentrates the necessary force for movements and revolts, it becomes all the more magnificent and glorious.

Here again, as always, the poems of the proletarian poets reflect the deepest notes of their aims and aspirations. The industrial city with its gigantic technical creations will enable them to press forward toward freedom, communism, and the brotherhood of races. But to reach the goal they are striving for, to bring about the "flowery Eden" on earth, the efforts of the international proletariat must be concentrated. This can be attained, they believe, through the big cosmopolitan cities where workingmen of all nationalities are united like "brothers in work and want," and where there is always a joyful hopefulness for the revolt against the "tyrants of old." And so the cities, which bear in themselves fire, impulse, and force resound again and again in their verse.

> O cities, O cities!
> I am born 'mid the fire of work,
> I am going there,
> There,
> Where Russian, German, Magyar, French, and other brothers,
> Flinging their curse relentlessly at the tyrants of old,
> Hardened with callouses, crossing Rubicons forever,
> From pole to pole, like one man, arise in revolt.
> In the heat of the tumult I am not on the scaffold,
> I am not crucified, like the black foe;
> I will joyfully enter the sword-armed circles
> Of the callous hand, of the great brotherhood,
> Of the native dawn and the new rising sun.

I will say prayers to beauty, to glory I will sing hymns,
And with my brothers, scarred, always at work and in want,
With strong steely muscles, with drops of sweat and blood,
Forward, forward
I shall go.

O cities!
On the road of grief and joy,
Of need and heavy toil,
Amidst the workmen's want
That roars with wrath like the ocean,
Like them, I shall trample
The flowers of cultured taste,
Bnt without losing my reason in the battle.
In the heat of revolt
I shall not forget
To weave my poems
Into the invisible wreath of art.

O cities!
What are drops of sweat?
What is revolt to me?
On my brow you see
Not only drops of sweat
And the scars of an uprising,
Not only deep furrows,
Scorched with fever
Of work and suffering,
But passionate desire
To be in the revolt,
To kindle a universal fire.   —*Malashkin.*

It is evident that not only the city but the very imagination of the proletarian poets is possessed by a whirling
motion. Revolt and a universal uprising are their highest
aims. Hence in their great hymn to the city, their hearts
turn away from tranquility and poise and seek the path

to tumultuous passions. Poets of a social revolution that was the signal of a new faith, the faith of materialistic science, they go on fighting for it undauntedly. Doing away with all old standards, seeking to destroy the capitalistic state and the "cultured taste" of the *bourgeoisie* they are endeavoring to establish a new system of esthetics, new conceptions of beauty, of architecture, of art.

> O poets and esthetes, curse the Great Destroyer!
> Kiss the fragments of the past lying under your heels,
> Wash the ruined temples with your tears!
> We live for a different beauty. . . . .
>
> —*Kirillov.*

From the imaginings of this "different beauty" and of the "future flowery Eden" the proletarian poets derive much of the vigor that fills their poems. The road to the perfect order, to the brotherhood of races may be a thorny one, it may cause "grief and heavy toil," but to them it does not seem impossible to traverse. For in the modern city with its cosmopolitan conglomeration a unified race is already in the process of making. Moreover, the same "ardent desires" fire the workers of all the countries of the world. And since to the proletarian poets desire and reality are not far apart, they already see the international proletariat united by one common cause, imbued with one common energy. Hence their vision that the mighty city "clad in emerald and steel," that enchanted place whence come all the wonders of science, will give them strength enough to break through all barriers, to overcome all obstacles, and to bring "the flowery Eden" to all humanity.

CHAPTER XII

CONCLUSION

In the preceding chapters I have tried to present as objectively as possible the spirit, the thoughts, the moods, and the aspirations, of the peasant and the proletarian poets. In the following few pages I wish to lay stress upon the most salient features of their poetry and to add certain observations essential for the understanding of its value.

A glance through the poems here given will suffice to show that the only notable feature common to the works of the peasant and proletarian bards is the infinite enthusiasm with which they celebrate the November revolution. The thought of their liberation from the old régime, in which they saw the absolute cause of their sordid life, fills all these poets with cheerfulness and joy: the strings of their hearts vibrate and sing. On all other subjects, however, their opinions clash, their psychologies diverge, and their ideals become diametrically opposed.

The proletarian poetry, born in a time of great political and social events, is permeated with the spirit of agitation and unrest. Produced amid the clang and uproar of revolutionary outbreaks, it resounds like the thundering echo of a volcano in eruption. Vehement in its tone and accent, passionate and energetic in its expression, it throbs with a fever which seems almost madness. Its range is very limited; there is no variety in its themes. Patriotism and individualism disappear and its avowed objects are internationalism and communism. Though there are many excellent single poems, yet, taken as a whole, this proletarian poetry possesses no striking originality, nor any profound depth. Inspired by the teachings of scientific socialism, it reflects no human feelings which lie beyond the range of that science.

The proletarian poets, instilled with the pride of victors, have swept aside all the old institutions and traditions, without troubling to discriminate between the good and the bad. In their poems they show no attachment whatever to the ancient Russian culture, which is to them nothing but an atavistic remnant. Religion, they proclaim, is a curse, for it helps the *bourgeois* class to befog the reason of the masses. Thus the centuries-old Russian Orthodoxy, in which the very soul of the nation had found expression, becomes to them "an accursed past." Their supreme faith is materialism. From this shallow belief they derive the power and the boldness to raise themselves to the height of "men-gods," to judge and to condemn the order of the universe.

Notwithstanding the forceful tone with which the proletarians sing the revolution, the struggle of classes, the might of the factory and the city, and the communistic millenium, their poetry does not possess qualities of lasting value. Its link with the past is negligible. Furthermore, it does not even bring out the essential traits of the Russian character. Such arrogant utterances as "We can," "We may," "We are all, we are in all," "We are Titans," "We are superior to God," etc., are by no means characteristic of the humble and fatalistic Russian masses. Not one of the proletarian poets gives us in his works a real and familiar image of Russia. The materialistic philosophy which controls and rules their minds has blurred the face of their mother country. Their songs are but the expression of an eventful moment, an exulting cry of tormented and revolted souls, and they are valuable only as a record of proletarian ecstasy in time of revolution.

The peasant poetry, though it, too, was produced in the midst of revolutionary upheavals, is less noisy and more profound than that of the proletarians. It is saturated with a divine spirit; it keeps alive the ideals and experiences of their race. Its outstanding features are religion, love of country, and veneration for past traditions. It embodies the essential traits of the national character and reveals the good and the bad in the Russian temperament. Nature shines forth in it in all her magic and beauty. In its supreme exaltation of the spiritual above the material, it represents something that has always been and that always will be of everlasting value in Russian literature.

Religion is the main storehouse from which the peasant poets draw their themes and their ideas of the meaning of life. The powers of evil may at certain moments be in the ascendancy, but these poets are convinced that in the process of time divine justice must come to its own. Thus, despite the attempts made by the present atheistic government to eradicate religion and to enslave the masses to materialistic theories, the peasants, unlike the proletarians, continue to preserve steadfastly the unadulterated faith of their fathers. This is abundantly illustrated in their poems. Their humble reverence before the power that is above men, and their tenacious holding to their faith in Christ and in the divine order of the universe, widely differentiate them from the proletarians. And it is this religious attitude that links spiritually all the peasant poets to the old Russia.

If we turn from the peasant poets' conception of their inner life to their notions of things around them, we find that here also they represent the tastes and predilections of the best prerevolutionary Russian writers. They despise the oppressive atmosphere and the feverish activity of the cities and factories. They like to fix their glances upon the quiet villages, where, in calm contemplation, they can enjoy the faint murmurs of their native air and fields. Like most of their predecessors they sing with fulness of feeling the charm and simplicity of rural life. Their poems on nature are the finest of all. One feels in them the sensitiveness and the touch of real artists. These peasants feel deeply the forlornness and sadness of the Russian landscape. Their peaceful and melancholy pictures, their impressions of fields, rivers, woods, and sky, arouse in the heart of every Russian a poignant emotion.

In spite of the active communistic propaganda carried on by the Bolsheviks in present-day Russia, the peasant poets remain essentially individualists. There is no collective "We" in their poetry, nor is there any internationalism, which indeed they regard as a great menace to the prosperity of their country. Nurtured as their poetry is on the teachings of the Orthodox Church, it preserves what is best in the Russian traditions. It stands out from all the literary productions of their time by its sincere faith in God and by the melody of its language. All this makes it a part of the past and gives to it an element of permanency.

The raging floods of the revolution will subside. The current of life will again run its normal course in the land of suffering and tears. But there will hardly be a complete return to the past, no matter how pathetic and disappointing this thought may be to many a Russian. The communistic spirit which in the last decade has affected Russian art and literature is but a temporary phase, an unhealthy growth, reared in a close atmosphere of rebellion, hate, and vengeance. The proletarian poets, unless they change their conceptions and free their verses from their pompous verbosity, will gradually fall into oblivion. But it may safely be predicted that such will not be the fate of the peasant poets. So long as Russia shall exist in the vastness of her steppes, in the melancholy of her landscapes, in the sadness of her songs, and in the beauty of her language, so long will their poems move deeply the hearts of the Russian people and appeal strongly to their innermost souls.

APPENDIX

SELECTED POEMS AND
BIOGRAPHICAL NOTES

ALEXANDROVSKY, VASILI DMITRIEVICH

(b. 1897)

The son of a peasant from Baskakovo, a village in the province of Smolensk, Alexandrovsky was educated in an elementary school. At the age of eleven he began to earn his living in the local tannery. His further intellectual training consisted mainly in reading the classic Russian authors. Among contemporary writers Gorky has exercised a great influence upon the young poet. In 1916 Alexandrovsky served in the army and was sent to the front.

Alexandrovsky's first verse appeared in 1913, in a Moscow magazine, *The Living World*. His recent works are to be found in various Russian periodicals.

FROM THE "OCTOBER" CYCLE

Ring with thy blue snowflakes, October,*
Sing with the rustle of banners in our exultant hearts—
After the grave and the funereal chants
We shall have our everlasting feast.

Today there are red carnations in our souls,
There are iron and granite in our muscles today;
Like a sentinel, fire-faced October stands
At the entrance into the sunny days.

Struggle and Labor are with us, everywhere and forever;
O, those twins, tanned with the sun!
With steely voices they announce
Glad tidings to the ends of the Earth.

Today, remembering the Past,
The lover clings to his beloved—
Many a life this night has devoured,
Under the bygone yoke much strength was squandered.....

Ring with thy blue snowflakes, October,
Sing with the rustle of banners in our exultant hearts—
After the grave and the funereal chants
We shall have our everlasting feast.

---

* The Bolshevik Revolution took place on October 25, old style, November 7, new style. In the following poems the term "October" is used synonymously with the word "revolution."

THE STRUGGLE

My soul, louder thou must cry,
Strike the nerves of those asleep.
A skilful pilot is Time—
Toward the flaming heights it steers.

Pierce the drum of space,
Crush the stones, my feet—
There is no distance in the universe,
There is no beaten course.

A winged hurricane we have awakened,
And with shells we have ploughed the fields:
We demand full payment
For the centuries, killed by sleep.

We have summoned death for a moment,
To burn the putrefied past . . . .
Of steel are our sword and hands,
The earth is our crematory.

To beg for mercy is shameful,
If the new world is not welcome to you,
Go beyond life's wall,
Cover yourself with the earthly pall.

. . . . My soul, louder thou must cry,
Strike the nerves of those asleep.
A skilful pilot is Time—
Toward the flaming heights it steers.

THE PROLOGUE

When the blazing whip of the sun
Drove into the fog's back,
With handfuls of bloody records did we bespatter
All the pages of the Bible and the Koran.

Impudent like the flame of October,
Persistent like the strokes of an engine's wheels—
Neither seas nor hills, nor sleet,
Neither frost nor drought will stop us on our way.

We have come to trample Yesterday
Under the boots shod with anger,
To scatter fires like a golden fan,
To scourge bogs with the starry grain.

'Tis only the beginning—the prologue.
After us—are our children;
They will pave by the hundred new roads
Toward the shores of the Future Age.

No, they cannot, they cannot be silent—
These bells above the virgin land.
They are the hearts that 'gainst copper beat,
Bleeding with the life-giving sun.

More than the first hundred is broken to bits,
More than the first thousand is torn to tatters;
And the eyes burn below in the pit,
And the wolfish jaws chatter.

Not now, not now to cherish
In our souls the dreams of love,
Rather have we come to sing with our warm blood
A requiem mass to the past age.

Not now, not now do we seek
For rest on the beloved breast;
Mortal anguish will wring out
The gentle caress with an icy hand.

No, they cannot, they cannot be silent—
These bells above the virgin land—
They are the hearts that 'gainst copper beat,
Bleeding with the life-giving sun.

ARSKY, PAVEL ALEXANDROVICH

(b. 1886)

Arsky was born of poor parents in a small village of the province of Smolensk. When he was ten years old the family moved to the city of Poltava, in the Ukraine. His father gave him the rudiments of an education, and the boy soon became passionately fond of poetry. His favorite poets were Heine, Goethe, Schiller, Byron, Shakespeare, Pushkin, and Lermontov.

At the age of fifteen Arsky left his home, and entered upon a life of adventure. He was in turn a sailor, a mason, a miner. At the same time he belonged to various self-educating circles of workingmen. In 1905 he was arrested for spreading revolutionary propaganda. After his escape from the prison in Sebastopol, Arsky settled down in St. Petersburg, where he resumed his studies. In 1914 he was enlisted in the Pavlovsky regiment.

Arsky's works appeared for the first time in 1917, in Petrograd, in the *Red News* and the *Petrograd Pravda*. Since 1918 his stories and verse have been published by the *Petrograd Proletkult*. In 1924 he completed *Calvary*, a tragedy.

THE COLLECTIVE WILL

We are not alone, we are the flowing current . . . .
In the whirl of fiery suns,
Like a constellation, joyful and ardent,
In the mist of dead days we burn.

Scattering flames and thunders
We call to sedition, to revolt . . . .
Fire, water, iron, stone, and all,
All are submitted to us in this world.

We are free as the wind in the field,
In bondage we will never be;
Aflame are the wires of steel
With the fire of our great will.

We are passion, we are power, we are motion,
We are an impulse, we are a boisterous thought . . . .
Over all, and without exception
Reigns the mighty and terrible "Collective."

We bring light and revelation
To the world from the depth of the ages . . . .
We are the joyful hymn of redemption
In honor of depraved slaves.

We have destroyed the prison vaults
That we may see the glittering fields:
All the peoples are united with us,
The family of workmen throughout the world.

THE SONG OF THE HAMMER

In the smithies—red
And like Vesuvius menacing,
In the glitter of turquoise lightning,
We forge without rest,
And a sonorous song we sing,
As in the heat of a battle's alarm
We stamp and grind,
And ceaselessly gild with light
The darkness of night.
In the hour of anxiety, in the weary hour
Our friend is—laughter;
And the thundering bellows
Are our throaty singers.
'Tis no wind
That blows through the sails;
With young voices resounds
Our free and joyous chorus.
'Tis no rumbling of a distant tempest—
'Tis the formidable anvil and hammer
That have begun their fiery contest.
When iron is touched by the hammer,
The ringing echo groans,
And the echo sinks into the air,
Then with a clear and yearning trill,
Gently tinkling like a reed,
The steel rings and moans . . . .
Perhaps for help it summons?
With smoke the windows are curtained,
And as if shouting an answer
With a bright flame the furnace spurts forth;
And crimsoned with the rallying banner,
We forge with joy and cheer,
And the golden gems we scatter.
To work we summon ever;
We are lords, we are titans
Ruling over fire and iron.

ARTAMONOV, MICHAIL DMITRIEVICH

(b. 1888)

Artamonov's father was a landless peasant of the province of Kostroma, and for many years he earned an insufficient livelihood as a church warden and as a forest guard. The boy spent a lonely childhood in a log cabin in the woods. Upon graduation from elementary agricultural school he spent some years working in different factories. During the war he served in the army and was wounded.

Artamonov began publishing his works when he was only eighteen years old. In 1913, in the city of Ivanovo-Vosnesensk, he edited a literary weekly, *Smoke*, which was prohibited by the government. Several volumes of his verse were published in Petrograd from 1913 to 1919.

THE RASPBERRY WEST

The raspberry West
In the distance pales.
The sorrowful shades
Cover the earth.

Dreadful in the early morn
Is the rumble of cannon . . . .
There the raspberry glow
Has sunk away.

There the temples are not like churches,
The houses are not like dwellings;
And darkness and cold
Have shrouded the earth.

Whether it is a wood, or a town,
Or a road over boggy ground—
In the night's darkness
One does not know.

As if black steel
Had bound us,
Quietly, in silence,
We march into the distance.

The dawns and lightnings
Tremble in the skies:
Sorrowful Galicia's
Villages are afire.

BERDNIKOV, YAKOV PAVLOVICH

(b. 1889)

A native of Vanovo, in the province of Tambov, the son of a peasant family, Berdnikov attended the rural parish school, the courses in which, however, he did not finish. At the age of ten he began to earn his living in a factory. A year later his parents moved to St. Petersburg, where the boy was employed at various factories. While thus occupied he became involved in a "political affair" and was sentenced to exile. Upon his return to St. Petersburg he once more became a factory hand.

It was then that he took up his pen. Berdnikov's first verse appeared in 1912, in the newspaper *Pravda*. Since that time he has brought out several collections of verse, published in Leningrad and Moscow.

NEVER

In the storms the wires ring
Of terrible confusion.
For the black host there is no salvation
From the workmen's revolution;
For the black host there is no salvation,
And never will there be!

Never! roar the factories,
Never! hiss the belts.
We will disperse misfortune's gloom,
Death to tyrants in the days of freedom,
In the volcanic days!

Still the cries and groans
In the dust, in the suffocating factories!
We are not slaves, but legions
Who have raised the banners,
We are the Children of Earth and Sun.

Not for a prayer have we come;
We have left our murky dens
For a dreadful, bloody fight;
We are strong, we are free. . . .

Not in vain:
Powerfully, proudly,
The serfs of labor
Have stirred many a summit and plain,
Boats and towns. . . . .

In storms the wires ring
Of the red revelation:
For the black host there is no salvation,
For the black host there is no salvation,
And never will there be!

BEZYMENSKY, ALEXANDRE ILLYCH

(b. 1898)

A native of the city of Zhytomir, in southern Russia, Bezymensky has been a member of the Bolshevist party since 1917. He is also one of the organizers of the "October" group of poets, who have a great reverence for the Bolshevik revolution.

His first attempt at writing was made in 1918. His three volumes of works appeared from 1920 to 1923.

TODAY

Today
The city streets
Are bursting forth with crowds.
Today
The shores
Are overflowed with human souls.
Today
The last ladders
And bridges of the past are burnt.
Today
The weakest
Is the power in a free land.
Today
Hearts thump
In the proud chest—the drum.
Today
In every buttonhole a bloody bow
Glares like the sun.
Today—
But not only for today!
The walls of boundaries have crumbled.
Today
For thoughts—the birds
The heavens are vaulted
With posters.
Today in the inferno
The points of starry nails are forged!
Glory to thee, today!
The mother of the days of tomorrow!

BEDNY, DEMYAN (pseudonym)

(b. 1883)

Efim Alexandrovich *Pridvorov* was born at the village of Gubovka, in the province of Kherson. The first seven years of his life he spent with his father at Elizavetgrad, where the latter was employed as a church warden. Thereafter the boy lived for some years with his mother in a village, where he received some scanty education. At the age of fourteen he attended the military first-aid surgical school. Upon his graduation he served in the army. In 1904 he passed his matriculation examinations and entered the Historico-Philological College of the University of St. Petersburg. During the great war he was an assistant surgeon in the army. The Civil War found him in the ranks of the Red Army. For his devotion to the cause, as a poet and a soldier, he was presented with the badge of the Red Banner.

Demyan Bedny's first public appearance as an author was made in 1909, when his verses were published in the Socialist monthly *Russkoe Bogatstvo* and later in the radical newspaper *Zvezda*. The numerous works he has written since then consist mainly of fables, satirical verse, and stories.

THE WORKMEN'S HYMN

Su, Fratelli, su, compagne . . . .

Rise, ye brothers; rise, ye sisters!
To the ranks, ye steel-tempered fighters!
The light of the Future's sun
Already shines on the banner of crimson.

Degraded and imprisoned
We have boldly sworn to fight
For our cause; in our ranks
There's no room for treason.

Has Labor been freed from its bitter fate
By the Children of Toil
That the shackles of bondage
May bind us again? Never, Never!

Mines, factories, foundries
Have maimed us and bent—
By the nobility, like beasts of burden,
We were hitched to a plough.

Those at whose will we perished
Left us no bread, but promised—
The grace of heaven
On the last Day of Judgment.

Capital's cursed burden
Has doomed us to torment,
Our hands were constrained
To till the stranger's land.

Let the flail and the plough
Still the hatred amongst men!
Let our life be adorned
With justice and love!

In unity is our strength;
While single—each one is a pariah!
The world's heart—the proletariat—
We are the levers of the universe!

All that is—is our creation:
We will destroy, we will rebuild.
Forward then, with a bold step!
Let all the foes perish!

The foes are no strangers to us.
Only the rich need boundaries;
We are free like the birds,
And we shall rebuild the world:

We will proclaim death upon the kingdom of death!
Death to the camarilla of masters!
The sword of violence—'gainst violence!
Our motto is: Make war upon war!

Curses on him who feasts,
If at that moment in the world
There still exist a single pauper
Who has lost his bread and roof.

Curses on laughter
If in the world remain a single tear!
Thrice cursed is he who speaks of peace
When in the clutches of his foes.

Our sisters and helpmates
In work and misery,
Ye, who to the tyrants gave
Your blood and your beauty.

Do not caress the low poltroons,
Rascals of the aristocratic cabal.
Without firm brotherly union
Our host will waver in the first battle.

If the faith in equality and fraternity
Is not a lie, or a wicked jest,
If the rebellion is not a blasphemy,
Then the struggle is not madness.

Strengthen ye, brothers and sisters,
The power of Labor over capital.
To give way to the foe in the least
Is the wretched slave's cowardice.

Has Labor been freed from its bitter fate
By the Children of Toil
That the shackles of bondage
May bind us again? Never!
No, never! No, never, never!

DEYEV–HOMYAKOVSKY, GRIGORI DMITRIEVICH

(b. 1888)

Deyev-Homyakovsky was born at Homyakovka, a village in the province of Kaluga. His parents were poor and illiterate peasants. At the age of six the boy had to beg alms. In due time, however, he attended the primary school, from which he graduated when he was eleven years old. Thereafter for some years he was employed on various estates as a shepherd or a drover. During his early youth he came to Moscow, where he worked at a shoemaker's and later in a bakery. The sordid life in these shops made a grim impression upon him, and the only solace he found was in books. These were mainly on religious topics. As a lad of fifteen he went to a monastery, intending to become a monk and live a saintly life. He was disappointed in his expectations and returned to Moscow. In 1905 he began to study seriously, attended night school, and in 1909 passed the examinations for a country teacher. Later he was a student of the University of Shanyavsky at Moscow.

He took up his pen when still working at the bakery. His first poems and short stories were published in 1907 in such magazines as *Rodina, Iskra, Zhivoe Slovo,* etc. A volume of his works appeared in 1912, and several others from 1919 to 1923.

THE PEASANTS' MARCH

Do not wake those who are asleep,
The dawn has blushed with a crimson deep.
March ye all who trust the men of toil,
Our heritage we are destined to foil.

> The moon reigns o'er the dark,
> O'er the day lords the sun,
> With scarlet banners our march we start.

Too long we were a trade for the tyrants,
Lulled to sleep by the clergy and merchants,
For the nobility, like cattle we were herded;
Grandfather and father with a knout were murdered.

> The moon reigns o'er the dark,
> O'er the day lords the sun,
> With scarlet banners our march we start.

The age of parasites is past;
Workmen and peasants perished fast;
Their huts were not thatched,
The cot and the field in their need were matched.

> The moon reigns o'er the dark,
> O'er the day lords the sun,
> With scarlet banners our march we start.

Now the new sun is rising
Over the great land of the peasants;
Into our little window it is bravely shining,
The hale and singing spring is with us.

The moon reigns o'er the dark,
O'er the day lords the sun,
With scarlet banners our march we start.

The red banners flutter loftily
Over the ricks of our native fields,
And the mighty flame of liberty
Bright light for our hamlets yields.

The moon reigns o'er the dark,
O'er the day lords the sun,
With scarlet banners our march we start.

We shall build a new edifice
For Labor—with no knouts nor whips—;
'Tis the end of all our griefs:
We will summon the parasites to justice.

The moon reigns o'er the dark,
O'er the day lords the sun,
With scarlet banners our march we start.

DRUZHININ, PAVEL DAVIDOVICH

(b. 1890)

The son of a peasant of the province of Penza, Druzhinin's childhood years were spent in dire poverty. His parents were illiterate and his father, addicted to drink, passed away when the boy was barely eight years old. After two years of school he went to work at the local match factory, earning eight or ten copecks a day. At the age of fifteen he ran away to Moscow. From 1905 until 1911 he lived a sort of semi-nomadic life, working whenever it was possible to find employment. This is what the poet says of these years: "A dreadful, heart-rending agony oppressed my soul: it was painful to look upon such human deformity, upon such poverty and filth, amid which the people were stifled, and passed away uttering curses against those who were well fed and piggishly contented." The only escape from this nightmare the young Druzhinin found in books.

The appearance of Gorky's *Emelyan Pilai* was a stimulus to his own attempts at writing. His first verse, "My Brother," was printed in 1910 in the newspaper *Dolya Bednyaka* ("The Pauper's Lot"). He has two volumes of verse to his credit, published in 1920 and in 1924.

THE TILLER

Disheveled and tousled—I am a peasant
Smelling of the green mint.
For thee—my virgin land
All the livelong day I long.

Thee—my fallow field,
My joy, my sweat and blood,
All my life long did I bemoan
Standing at the gates in times of flood.

How often I have paced thee
Only I and my battered jade know.
As if amidst the flames, my soul
Lives in this callous hand.

With every grass blade, with every ear of wheat
Lived and thought the tiller;
His hair is turned white with grief;
Grief has bleached his furrowed brow.

Like his old red shirt
His body—a mere shade—is worn.
But naïve is the tiller's faith;
Like the first day, the age's firstborn.

In the bloody fight I pine;
Into the fields, tender and meek, I go,
And with a prayer, as of old,
To kiss thee, my earth, I come.

ESSENIN, SERGYEY ALEXANDROVICH

(1895–1925)

Essenin came of a destitute peasant family of the province of Ryazan. From his second year he was brought up by his grandparents. Later he was sent to a parish boarding school from which he graduated at the age of sixteen. It was intended to send him on to the Moscow Teachers' Institute, but Essenin tells us in his autobiography: "Fortunately this never came to pass. I was so fed up with the methods of teaching and didactics that I did not want to hear any more of them." His life career came to an end in 1925, when on December 28 he committed suicide.

He began to write poetry at the tender age of nine, but his first printed verse appeared when he was seventeen. At eighteen he came to St. Petersburg, where he met Alexander Blok and a few other contemporary writers. During 1916–1925 ten volumes of his verse were published.

THE WOLF'S PERIL

The world of mystery, my ancient world,
Like the wind thou art calm and silent.
Thine aged throat is strangled
By the strong hands of the pavement.

The ringing dread hurls itself
Upon the whiteness of the snow.
I welcome thee, my black peril,
To meet thee, I go!

O city, city! In a cruel combat
Thou hast christened us a carrion and a curse.
Gagged with the telegraph poles
The field in deep anguish grows cold.

The devil's neck has muscles like sinews,
And the cast-iron beams are not heavy for it.
Ah, well! To us it is not news
That we have tottered and perished.

Let the heart be heavy, let it burn,
'Tis a song of the rights of the beast.
Thus, chased by the hunters, the wolf
Is ensnared in the trap, is brought to bay.

The beast is crouching .... and from the dim cave now
Someone will pull the trigger ....
A sudden leap .... and the biped foe
With the wolf's tusks is torn.

O my beloved beast, I welcome thee!
Not for nothing to the knife thou succumbed.
Everywhere pursued—like thee
Amid the iron foes I pass.

Even like thee, I am ever on the alert,
And though the triumphant horn I hear,
In my last victorious deadly leap
I will taste my foe's blood.

And upon the soft whiteness let me fall
And sink into the snow . . . .
Upon the other shore there will be sung
My peril's vengeance song.

I BELIEVE

I believe, I do believe: there is happiness.
The sun has not yet set.
Like a red prayer-book are the skies
Which predict the glad tidings.
I believe, I do believe: there is happiness.

Ring and peal, thou golden Rus!
Blow, thou turbulent wind!
Blest is he who looked with cheer
Upon thy pastoral sadness.
Ring and peal, thou golden Rus!

I love the rumble of stormy seas
And the glitter of stars on the waves.
The blessed suffering,
And the blessing people . . . .
I love the rumble of stormy seas.

WHENEVER I GAZE

Whenever I gaze upon the field, upon the skies,
In the field and in the heavens there is paradise.
Again my virgin land
In the stacks of wheat is drowned.

Again there are countless herds
In the groves that were untrodden,
And from the mountains green
The golden water streams.

O, I believe it is for the tormented,
Ruined peasant
That the milk is poured down
By a gentle hand.

COMRADE

He was a simple workman's son,
His life's story is not long.
All he had—was his hair, as dark as night,
And his eyes—blue and mild.

His father from morn till night
Has bent his back—to feed the little one.
But there was nothing to do for the child:
He had two friends: Christ and a cat.

The cat was old and deaf,
He did not hear the flies nor the mice;
In the arms of his mother was Christ,
From the ikon he looked at the pigeons under the eaves.

Thus lived Martin, and nobody knew him.
Sadly, the days dropped, like rain on the iron;
Only seldom at a scanty dinner
To sing the Marseillaise his father taught him.

"You'll grow up," he said, "and comprehend,
Then you will guess why we are so poor."
His broken knife dully trembled
'Gainst the stale crust of daily bread.

But then under the shattered
Windows
Two winds fluttered
Their wings;
Thus with the springtide
Flood
The people of Russia
Saw blood.

> The ramparts rumble,
> There sings the thunder!
> In the blue darkness
> Eyes sparkle!

Sweep after sweep,
Corpse after corpse.
Fear breaks
Its strong teeth.

> Again an upward flight, again!
> A cry again and then another!
> Into the bottomless mouth
> The stream flows . . . .

And then for somebody struck
The last sad hour . . . .
Trust ye, he did not cower
Before the strength of hostile eyes.

> His soul, just as of old,
> Is strong and bold,
> Toward hope his bloodless hand
> Is stretched out.

Not in vain did he live,
Not in vain did he the flowers crumple;
But you do not resemble
The dead dreams. . . . .

Unforeseen and sudden, from Martin's home porch
His father's last cry reached forth.

With dimmed eyes and frightened bluish lips
The cold corpse he embraced, and fell on his knees.

Then his eyebrows twitched, he dried his eyes with his hand;
Into the hut he ran and stood before the ikon.

"Jesus, Jesus, hearest Thou? Seest Thou? Alone I am!
I call Thee and need Thee, I am thy friend Martin."

"Father lies there—killed, not like a coward did he fall!
O my true Jesus, I hear—for us is his call!"

"He summons us to help the Russian people in the struggle,
He tells us to fight for freedom, equality, and labor!"

> Kindly did he hearken
> To the innocent words,
> Christ descended upon the earth
> From the immovable arms.
>
> They walk shoulder to shoulder,
> And the night is black and dark.
> The gray silence
> Bristles with misfortune.
>
> With hope their dreams blossomed
> Toward the immortal and free destiny.
> Their eyelids were caressed
> By the breeze of February.
>
> Suddenly . . . . there flashed fire . . . .
> The copper charges barked . . . .
> And pierced with bullet
> Fell Jesus the Child.
>
> Listen:
> There is no more resurrection,
> His body was taken and buried:
> He lies
> On the field of Mars.
>
> And where his mother did remain,
> He will never come again;
> There by the window,
> The old cat
> Catches the moon with his paw.

On the floor crawls Martin:
My falcons, dear falcons,
You are in prison,
In prison!

His voice grows faint and dull,
Somebody crushes him, strangles him,
And fire scorches him.

But beyond the window
The iron word
Is quietly singing,
Then dying, then flashing anew:
Re—pub—lic!

O MY DEAR FIELDS

O my dear fields and furrows,
How beautiful are you in your sadness!
I love these shabby little huts
With the waiting gray-haired mothers.

I will throw myself at the feet shod with bast:
Peace be with you, rake, scythe, and plough!
By the gaze of the bride I guess
The fate of the groom in the war.

With humble thoughts I am at peace,
I long to be a shrub by the water.
To the evening star burning a taper
With the womenfolk I shall hope for the better.

I have guessed their numberless thoughts
That neither thunder nor dark will frighten,
Behind the plough and with sacred songs
One will not think of death or prison.

They believed in these scrawls
That were written with so much pain,
They wept with joy and happiness
As at the first rain after a drought.

On the soft grass, under the beady dew,
With their thoughts of the departed kin,
They dream of the hazy meadows
And the merry hay-making season.

O thou Rus, my meek mother country!
My love is only for thee!
Merry is thy brief happiness
With a loud song on the meadows in spring.

AGAIN THE CART RUMBLES

Again the crude cart rumbles,
And the shrubs and the plains run by.
Along the road there are chapels again
And the memorial crosses for the dead.

I am ill again with a feverish grief
From the fragrance of oats in the breeze,
And toward the belfry's whitewash
My hand involuntarily makes the sign of a cross.

O Rus, the raspberry plain,
The azure sunk in the stream.
I love with ecstasy and pain
Thy sorrow, like the lake, crystalline.

One cannot fathom thy cold grief;
On a misty shore thou art,
But not to love thee, not to trust thee—
That I cannot do, I cannot master.

I shall not give up these fetters,
I shall not part with my long dream,
When the native steppes ring
With the whisper of feather-grass prayers.

ACROSS THE FIRST SNOW I RAMBLE

Across the first snow I ramble,
In my heart—the white lily of the awakening might,
O'er my path the star is lighted at night
Like a blue candle.

I know not whether it is light or dark,
Whether in the thicket the wind howls, or the cock crows.
In the fields there is perhaps no winter,
It is only the swans in the meadows.

O white plain, thou art full of beauty!
My blood tingles with light frost!
I long to press to my body
The birches' naked breasts.

O, the woody and dense darkness!
O, the joy of snow-clad fields!
My arms are hungry for an embrace
Of the willows' wooden thighs.

O THOU, MY DARLING RUS

O thou, my darling Rus,
Thy cots are like the gilt-framed ikons . . . .
There is no verge, no border to gaze on,
And the eyes imbibe the distant blues.

Like a pilgrim I go hence,
And look upon these fields of thine;
Yonder by that low fence
The tinkling poplars pine.

Apple and honey perfumes,
In churches thy humble Redeemer—
And echoing the season's tunes
The meadows drone with merry dancers.

I'll run along the trodden bent
Into the wealth of green jungle;
To welcome me, like a catkin,
Will the maiden's laughter tinkle.

If the heavenly host should decree:
"Forsake thy Rus and live in Eden,"
"No paradise·for me," I'll say then,
"Give back my country to me."

IN A HUMBLE MONK'S COWL

In a humble monk's cowl,
Or simply a towhead beggar,
To those plains I shall go
Where milk from the birches flows.

I want to fathom all the earth,
My guide will be the twinkling star.
And amid the field singing with rye,
In the happiness of my kin I want to believe.

The early morn with a cool dewy hand
Shakes down the apples of the dawn.
Raking the hay on the meadow
For me the peasants sing their song.

Looking beyond the bounds of the wattled fence,
With myself thus I spake:
"Happy is he who his life did adorn
With the scrip and the staff of a vagabond."

"Happy is he who lives in humble joy,
Who has no friend nor foe,
Who, passing by the village road,
To the hayricks and stacks will pray."

A DROUGHT

A drought has killed the sprouts,
The rye withers, the oats wilt:
The peasant maids across the field
Walk to the litany with banners along the furrows.

The parishioners stood at the thicket
Hiding their gnawing grief.
A puny priest did snuffle:
"Lord, save Thou thy people."

The heavenly gates did open,
With a woody might roared the deacon:
"Again pray with faith, O brethren,
That our Lord may drench the fields with rain."

The birds chirped a joyful strain,
The priest sprinkled handfuls of holy water,
The jabbering magpies, like match-makers,
Called in quest of rain.

Beyond the grove the quivering sunset foamed,
Like homespun linen rolled the clouds.
And faintly amid the parched plants
And shrubs the hazy river groaned.

Taking off their caps, praying and sighing,
Among themselves the peasants spake:
"Not so bad was the ripening rye,
But the dry days were its blight."

" 'Gainst the sleigh, drawn by a steed—the dark cloud,
The fiery breeching flapped .... Darkness and trembling ....
And the lads clad in homespun shirts did cry:
"Rain, rain, pour down upon our rye."

FILIPCHENKO, IVAN GURIEVICH

(b. ——)

Belonging to a peasant family of the province of Saratov, Filipchenko began his life career as a bookbinder. Later he attended the University of Shanyavsky in Moscow. In 1913 he was arrested for revolutionary propaganda, and while in prison he became a communist.

His first writings date back to his fourteenth year. He has to his credit two volumes of verse, published in Moscow in 1918 and 1923.

THE SUN FESTIVAL

The haughty brass is not the eagle's call,
The chiding bronze is not the pealing, tinkling bells;
Now the bells of the belfry do not resound,
The metal's clang with a dark night is bound.

The tambourines jingle
And the bugles ring—
The sounds are sharp, coarse, free;
They whirl clouds, living clouds;
They are forging rapture, are forging the sounds.

In reverberating hymns they worship
The sun, earth and verdure,
The flowers of the plains, the grass of rocky valleys;
They hum all day in the squares and alleys,
At the open windows of sleepless noisy workshops,
O'er the smoky factory, where with gloomy faces,
Immured in the ghastly ancient granite vaults,
Workmen bend their backs—row after row.

Without hesitation, without dismay,
Let the miners put their sharp mattocks away,
Let the weavers leave their noisy looms,
The smiths will at once throw their hammers down,
And like the Cossacks stop their steeds;
Let the factory whistles masterfully cease
Their melancholy tunes.

The trumpets blare;
Like fiery manes float the banners;
They flutter in the air;
The gust hampers their turbulent ardor
At the crimson hour when everywhere darkness is driven away,
Ready for the festival—loving and beautiful—the world has
     arisen.

The summons peals: "Unite and come together!"
In love with themselves, the oceans of the populace,
Intoxicated, ecstatic,
Overflow the fields and the meadows.

Ye great and mighty working throng!
There before us,
There for us tonight
The bonfires of the heavens will shine.
Dropping down on the green carpet
The bosom quivers with a passionate might.

For three hundred days not seeing the sun,
For three hundred days not seeing ourselves,
Now on a spring day brighter than the golden sun
We have come out into the open—
To the young we must show the horizon.

Upon our hearts knocks the sun;
The sun has arisen, the sun has arisen,
Its rays will warm
The old and the young
As before.

All is green, the southern sun
Is everywhere;
All is golden,
A brother for a brother,
A friend for a friend,
A friend for the sake of his friend.

Call each other
And get together
For joy and play:
Along the sidewalks and streets
The bards, scalds, and singers
Will take us to the camps, the fields,
Into the open space
To give our eyes a feast.
On the green grass
We shall have our repast.

THE MASSES

The name of red masses,
This buzzing labor and fiery achievements;
Everywhere—numberless, endless—
Everywhere, every hour, every moment,
They shout about you.

In countless things this name reverberates on earth:
In trees, in stones and metals,
In docks, factories, arsenals,
On the printing presses,
In the hidden and terrible depth
Of huge books, the magic books one reads,
The letters of prophetic name,
The letters set in golden type are aflame!
'Tis the name of the awakened masses.

The illumined trains of iron,
The black tempestuous roaring herd!
There are human comets
In the winged flights of wheels;
The rims are the bent backs of working Huns,
The millions of spokes are their outstretched arms.
They bray like asses
The terrible name of the masses,
The name of Colossus.

The dance of electricity on the heavens at night,
The brilliant advertisements, the poems of light,
The belfries, minarets, towers,
And the signboards of iron—
In sunshine, in lightning
They tell of the name of the masses,
Of the Democracy of all races.

O, the worldly masters
Know too well about them,
Their movement's raging storm and wild calls
Will sweep away forever the kings' crowns, the tsars' thrones,
Like the ocean waves breaking the granite walls.

The masses are the forges,
The masses are the furnaces, foundries;
Convulsively, persistently working,
Their paradise they are incessantly creating.

Hark, the distant whistles ring
With their iron hymn to the purple morn;
The city is asleep, the markets hardly stir,
But the masses are already afoot,
Raising powder-like dust
On the lanes and the streets.

The kerchiefs, overalls, flow like a river;
Masons, bricklayers in tawny aprons;
With knapsacks hurry the carpenters, sawyers,
Painters, with pails and forest of brushes;
All move with the clamoring throng.

There is the workroom;
Here is a row of iron weaving looms,
And a row of skilful weavers—women.
Their hands and figures gleam
Rhythmically in the movement of the levers;
Their eyes are aflame with burning thirst,
Their faces are deathly white
From the incandescent light
Arched in front of every one;
The factory feverishly weaves
For continuous delights and needs.

Clothing all the classes
With dresses of velvet, cloth, silk, linen;
Like the spring giving the trees a leafy attire,
There work the women of the masses
Inspired with their ardent desire.

There are the working masses
Of the gigantic factory—a stone bolthead,
Amidst the huge machines,
Amidst the senseless monsters' black herd,
Among their wheels, belts, shafts, levers, and springs;
Group after group of workmen
With heaps of treasures feed them,
Receiving things more wonderful than dreams.

There are a crowd of charred faces, cramped postures,
In the black shafts of coal,
In the pitchy dusk.
In galleries, adits, and drifts;
Bareheaded, roughly stripped,
Like cripples they crawl.
Everyone is crouching, fettered, with distended pupils;
They senselessly hammer the coal
With the pointed edge of a pick-axe,
With the blade of a mattock;
The leaping lights of crimson
Shine on their glossy bodies tense with motion.

Digging up the sun
From the black abysmal depths,
A pie filled with bodies and bones—the globe of the universe—
We fatten ourselves for a despotic employer.

In every smithy—
An ally in our destiny—
The blacksmiths at the furnaces
With a crimson light
On their chiseled faces,
On their bare arms and swinging black hammers,
On their prominent muscles, and strong stooping backs.
Powerfully strike
The anvils that are like iron rocks.

In wrath they smite
The metal—crumpled, crude, and white;
The sparks circle, like meteors in starry midnight,

Like thousands of stinging jaws the blows hiss and chide.
The caverns shudder,
The chasms wildly echo the passionate throes,
The infernal strokes on miles and miles of stone
In the dark vaults of the earth.
The hollows yell, gnash, and groan.

Every mile of space on the earth echoes;
All human backs are bent, necks are stretched,
Panting lips are parched.

The pavements, the black throats of the mines,
The mountains, the earth's crust, the towns
In America, Africa, Asia, and Europe,
In the east and west, in the south and north
Consumed with maddening fires,
Groan from dawn to dawn.

Everywhere hammer after hammer ceaselessly strikes
And forges its ideal with all its might;
Democracy is forging,
The masses are forging,
The masses persistently smite,
They shape from the granite,
They mould from steel and gold,
To the muffled sound of the red tocsin—
O, be praised—happiness for future ages.

The masses forge for themselves an eagle's fate,
They mould themselves in the crucible of the age
Into one superman;
They wish to be and they will become one titanic heart and
    mind;
At the iron furnace, turned white with heat,
This iron on the anvils will not cheat.

THE BLACKSMITH

More than once you were admired
By millions of kind eyes,
And the poets of the ages, of you—the boisterous one,
Have sung more than once.

But I, your young singer,
I am a blacksmith myself;
I can forge iron, and I am forging
And singing.

Not a few smithies I have known;
I have seen thousands and more of them;
From snowy Siberia to boggy Poland,
From fiery Caucasus to gloomy Finland,
To forge the metal, smithy after smithy
Has appeared
In a rapture of ecstasy.

On the anvils, as on a scaffold,
By the flaring furnaces,
The pieces of purple iron
Shrivel and bend, and wait for the creating hand
Of the blacksmiths
In coarse shirts and leather aprons.

There they rise—with turned-up sleeves;
They stoop to pick up their hammers,
Spit on their palms and half-clenched fists.
Throng after throng, mighty host after host,
They wait for the hour, the signal
To forge surpassing products.
The furnaces flare and throw purple light
Into the night
On the figures of smiths of primeval force.

They begin
Amid thunder and lightning.
An impetuous sweep
Of thousands and thousands of flying arms
Suddenly swinging
Their hammers upward in purple darkness.
Dz–b–o–o–m!

The sparks, like sand in a simoon;
The sparks, startled like a whirl of radiant rings,
Above their heads are like a crown,
And each profile is brown as bronze;
Like groups of beautiful sculpture,
In the glimmering reflection, every smith is cast.
At the tense moment of the stroke,
With huge muscles—a handsome, untidy creature—
He is all power, all movement in this iron sport;
While stooping, he throws down his hammer,
And straightening, he lifts it sparkling;
This one to the left, that one to the right,
In the red dusk, in bloody light,
In a file, they are forging
And singing:
It is boisterous here, it is turbulent here, where the metal we
    beat.
The long day, lifting hammer after hammer,
Is itself like the golden and fiery heat.
It is one of the bawlers;
Piercing the uproar, it booms like a tocsin.
We know, we know the whole country is virgin.
There is much work,
Iron work,
For all together—
Over the precipice
We are God's hammersmiths.

We forge, we forge another life,
We forge a life of steel;

Without fail we will make a golden life,
The flame, the light of an ideal
And the power of thought—the source of all
We shall mould as hitherto unknown;
For her—for life—we will forge!

Our muscles are strong,
The muscles of the united workmen's throng,
Of workmen's metal-like, creative hands,
Of the world's democracy—a body like a buffalo, and a spirit
    like a god.
The inevitable, the inevitable day is near,
And for us hammer after hammer,
The battle trumpet and the horn
Will prophetically proclaim
Aloud.
And the triumphant thunder from the clear skies
Shouts to this age forged by the masses:
He who is not a blacksmith is not a man.

FOMIN, SEMYON DMITRIEVICH

(b. 1881)

A native of the village of Sychevo in the province of Vladimir, Fomin received an elementary education and later devoted his time to self-improvement, attending evening courses at the People's University. The years 1912–1913 he spent in Switzerland, and upon his return to Russia he became a village teacher.

He began to write at sixteen. His first verse appeared in the *Novaya Volya* ("New Freedom"), 1907. Two volumes of his works were published by him in 1914 and 1920.

THE CALL OF THE EARTH

Away from the cities
I shall go to the fields, to the sun.
From the cup of thine azure skies
Give thy sacrament, O Earth.

There is nothing more prayerful, beautiful,
Than the hermit-huts in the ocean of rye,
When beyond the heated fields of purple
The incense is burnt by the pines.

Again I am a homeless pilgrim;
On the overflowed bank, beyond the river,
The radiant day I shall meet
With free songs of the village.

Where the earth drinks from the quiet stream
The fragrance of honey and rye,
There in the crimson quiver of sunrise,
My people, with thee I shall unite.

SHATTERED IKON

Shattered ikon,
Lacerated Russia mine!
My heart is broken,
And I pray for thee.

Before the scarlet blaze
Pales thy sorrowful face.
I have touched thy wounds,
Of a sudden thy secrets I fathom.

Thou art a fairy tale, a legendary song
In the glitter of everlasting stars.
Forgive me; like thy son
I will build a cross upon my past.

I trust and trust not,
I comprehend and yet I fear.
Before the world the gates opened
And a different Rus appeared.

From out the ashes of burning fever
Thou didst come forth alive;
A parable thou art,
From the east thou hast kindled the light.

GERASIMOV, MICHAIL PROKOFIEVICH

(b. 1889)

Gerasimov was born in a switchman's log cabin on the Zlatoust railway line. At the age of nine he helped his father, working on the embankments. He attended the Kinelsk primary school and later the technical school (belonging to the railway company) at Samara. In 1905 he became a member of the Social Democratic party, and in the following year he was arrested. While in prison he spent his time reading. After his release he devoted himself entirely to the cause of the party. In 1907 he fled through Finland to Europe. In Belgium, France, and other countries, he worked in mines, iron works and foundries and he was also employed as waiter, locksmith, and electrician. During his peregrinations he became, according to his own statement, "well acquainted with the prisons of France, Belgium, and Italy." When the great war broke out Gerasimov enrolled in the French army, but was sent back to Russia in 1915 for disobedience and for pacifist propaganda. In 1916 he was arrested at Samara. Since the revolution he has been entrusted with various responsible duties.

He began to write in 1913, and his first verses were published in the magazine *Prosveschenye* ("Enlightenment"). Since then he has brought out several volumes of poems.

IRON

There are groans in iron,
The clanging of gyves,
And the cry of guillotine knives;
And shrapnel shells
With a splatter fell
On the limits of the earth.

There are calls in iron
Full of tingling ire,
Of the flowing molten stream;
With the clamor of metal
Something stirs and rises,
Something sparkles in the depths of the eyes.

There is purity in iron,
There are luster and longing
Of the eyelashes, like Mimosa, tender;
There are trills of flutes
Which flash and vanish
In the smiles of exultant faces.

There is tenderness in iron,
The frolicking of snow-flakes;
And love glitters, when it is polished:
There is the crimson of sunset,
There are impulse and weariness,
And blood is on the rusty cleft.

There is autumn in iron,
The cold blueness
Amid the rusty pine twigs;
There is the scorching summer heat
Clad in a mirage
Of the fervent, flowering spring.

There is passion in iron,
There are turbulence and cadence
Of the waves splashing against rocks,
The siren's melody
In the seething foam,
Where the sinuous body is free.

There is forging in iron,
There are alertness and skill
In the dance of the callous hands.
There is a current in our veins
And in the ringing chisels;
In a foundry the circle is made.

There is might in iron:
Giants are reared
With the rusty juice of ore.
Like an iron host,
My brothers, march onward,
With the fiery banner of Labor.

WE SHALL TAKE ALL

We shall take all, we shall know all,
We shall pierce the depths to the bottom.
And drunk is the vernal soul
Like May, golden with blossoms.

To proud daring there is no limit,
We are Wagner, Leonardo, Titian.
On the new museum we shall build
A cupola like that of Montblanc.

In the crystal marbles of Angelo,
In all the wonder of Parnassus,
Is there not the song of creative genius
That like an electric current throbs in us?

Orchids were cultivated,
Cradles of roses were swung:
Were we not in Judea
When love was taught by Christ?

We laid the stones of the Parthenon,
And those of the giant pyramids;
Of all the Sphinxes, temples, Pantheons
We have cut the clanging granite.

Was it not for us that on Mount Sinai,
In the burning bush,
The Red Banner glowed, like the sun,
Amid storm and fire.

We shall take all, we shall know all,
We shall pierce the turquoise of the skies;
It is so sweet to drink on a blossoming day
From the life-giving showers.

IONOV, ILYA IONOVICH

(b. 1887)

Born at Odessa, in his childhood Ionov worked in a printing shop. Later he attended art school, but was expelled. In 1903 he was in prison for the first time, and in 1906 he was exiled to Siberia as a member of the Social Democratic party. In the following year he escaped from Siberia and soon after was arrested and sentenced to eight years of hard labor for belonging to the ''fighting organization'' of the Social-Revolutionary party. He served his term in the Shlusselburg fortress, in Pskov and in Orel. After the November revolution he managed the publications of the Petrograd Soviet, and at present is in charge of the State Publications (*Gosizdat*).

Ionov began his writing in 1905 in a clandestine newspaper *Proletarskoe Delo* (''The Proletarian Cause''). Two volumes of his verse have appeared in print, in 1917 and in 1921.

THE COMMUNISTS

(Dedicated to the members of the Russian Communist Party.)

Striving toward one great goal,
We know no fear in the struggle,
It was only we who in the year of grievous dole
Dared to confront our fate.
Whilst our foes
Their daggers in secret sharpened,
We sacrilegiously wrecked
The bounds of ancient laws.
Under our banners we have called
The family of the working commune;
With a sword we have traced the great road
Upon the map of the world.
That road is long. However steep be the climb
Toward the sunny summits,
Through fog and clouds, cold and dark,
We will carry our torchlight of red.
From our towers we already behold:
Across the sea,
O'er foreign fields and plains
The revolution's dawn is aflame.
From Moscow to New York
The resonant current runs
And with unseen hands
It writes the steely words:
"For the sake of the common fate of our brothers,
You, the proletarians of all the world,
With one strong will, one mighty effort
Rally to your great camp!
Rush to the rescue of communards,
Break serfdom's fetters,
Let the tumuluous tide scatter
At one sweep the old world."
The call is heard beyond the ocean,
The first loud peals resound.

Proud Albion, like a terrible tempest
May rise at any moment.
We are not alone . . . . Behold, ye brothers,
The same emblem across the sea:
The sheaf and the hammer, the plough and the sickle,
Are interlaced in one single embrace.

AT THE FOUNDRY

The steel claws of cranes rushed toward the ceiling
Hoisting with cables the finished engine;
It seems that now it will soar, proudly disappearing
In the maze of galleries, communicators, wheels.

The countless arches of cold sunshine
On the bronze muscles, making a sparkling hive.
Easy and light, like the galleys of an ancient host,
Like flaming serpents the cupolas float.

At the rails, writhing, stirring, like ants,
Are the fearless creators of unheard-of marvels;
And with a sure grasp the strong hands
Seize the hot handles of black levers.

Great eternal Labor! To thee be the praise,
With thy dew didst thou bathe us in the foundry's furnace;
With a masterly hand didst thou weld into a single rhythm
The slow beat of hearts and the rumble of anvils.

Perhaps, under the heavy blow,
Amidst the roar and babble of lathes one will fall;
Then we shall with more vigor, with the aid of muscles and steam,
Realize on earth the rich tapestry of dreams.

With the singing sharp drills and hissing locomotives,
In accord our work we shall do
Till the time when with the sound of different motives
Upon the new road we shall go toward the new.

KAZIN, VASILI VASILIEVICH

(b. 1898)

Kazin's parents were indigent peasants. He was born in Moscow and received his primary education at the elementary municipal school there. Later he entered the secondary school, where he was granted a scholarship. Upon his graduation he became interested in social activities. Shortly after the November revolution he participated in the organization of the "Third International."

His first verse appeared in 1914 in the *Penny Gazette*. He began his literary work in earnest only in 1918, when the *Proletkult* was established. Since then he has been a contributing member to the proletarian poets' magazines the *Gudki* ("Whistles") and the *Kuznitza* ("Smithy").

A volume of his verse was published in 1922; a second edition appeared in 1923.

THE HEAVENLY FACTORY

It is high and it is wide—
This blue stone factory.
Hark! The gusty blast
Calls with a dusty voice
And from all corners hurry
In thick sooty overalls
Throngs of stalwart smiths
Whom the windy blast has united.
Darker and darker are the vaults:
The black throngs meet
And quickly
They've kindled
The furnace of lightning
With sultry heat,
And with the roaring thunder
The factory walls shudder.

KIRILLOV, VLADIMIR TIMOFEEVICH

(b. 1889)

Kirillov is a native of Smolensk. His father was a peasant employed as a clerk in a bookstore. His early childhood was spent in a village, where for two years he attended the primary school. At the age of nine he worked as an apprentice to a shoemaker. Later he became a sailor in the Black Sea fleet. In 1907 he was arrested for his participation in the revolutionary uprising and was exiled for three years to the province of Vologda. Thereafter he traveled abroad for some time.

His first attempt at writing was made in 1908, while serving as a convict. Verse by him appeared in 1913 in the *Narodny Zhurnal* ("People's Magazine"). His col-lected works were published in 1924, in Moscow.

THE IRON MESSIAH

There he is—the saviour, the lord of the earth,
The master of titanic forces—
In the roar of countless steel machinery,
In the sparkle of suns of electricity.

We thought he would appear in a starry stole,
With a nimbus of divine mystery,
But he came to us clad in black smoke
From the suburbs, foundries, factories.

We thought he would appear in glory and glitter,
Meek, blessing and gentle,
But he, like the molten lava,
Came—multifaced and turbulent . . . .

There he walks o'er the abyss of seas,
All of steel, unyielding and impetuous;
He scatters sparks of rebellious thoughts,
And the purging flames are pouring forth.

Wherever his masterful call is heard,
The world's bosom is bared,
The mountains give way before him,
The earth's poles together are brought.

Wherever he walks, he leaves a trail
Of ringing iron rail;
He brings joy and light to us,
A desert he strews with blossoms.

To the world he brings the New Sun,
He destroys the thrones and prisons.
He calls the peoples to eternal fraternity,
And wipes out boundary lines.

His crimson banner is the symbol of struggle;
For the oppressed it is the guiding beacon;
With it we shall crush the yoke of destiny,
We shall conquer the enchanting world.

TO THE FUTURE

I have overheard these songs of years dear and joyful,
In the fire-faced and vast cities' roaring tumult.

I have heard these songs of the golden days of the future
In the factory turmoil, the clangor of steel, and the belts' wicked
    whisper.
I have looked at my comrade forging the golden steel
And then the wonderful face of the Future's Dawn I have seen.
I have learned that all the world's wisdom is in this hammer,
In this firm and stubborn and confident hand.

The harder the hammer beats, breaks, and forges,
The brighter will joy glitter in the gloomy world.

The swifter the commutators and trundles turn,
The more alluring and bright our days will burn.

These songs were sung to me by the voices of millions,
Millions of blue-bloused blacksmiths, brave and strong.

These songs are a rebellious call, a clear peal, masterful, red;
They tell all men that the long night's death-like sleep is ended.
These songs are a mighty call to the sun, to life and struggle;
To wicked and wearisome fate they are a proud and angry challenge.

WE

We are Labor's countless, unyielding legions.
We have conquered the expanse of seas, of land, and of ocean,
We have illumined towns with the light of artificial suns:
Our proud souls burn with a rebellious fire.

We are at the mercy of turbulent, passionate inebriety;
Let them shout: "You are the executioners of beauty,"
For the sake of our Tomorrow we will burn Raphael,
Destroy museums, trample the flowers of art.

We have thrown off the burden of oppressing inheritance,
We have renounced the chimeras of anemic wisdom;
The maidens in the Future's kingdom
Will be more beautiful than Venus.

Tears are dry in our eyes, gentleness is killed,
We have forgotten the fragrance of grass and flowers in spring,
We love the might of dynamite and the power of steam,
The song of sirens, the movement of shafts and wheels.

We have united with metal, our souls are fused in the machines,
We have forgotten to sigh and yearn for heaven;
We wish there were no more hungry on earth,
That there were no groans, nor cries for bread . . . .

O poets and esthetes, curse the Great Destroyer!
Kiss the fragments of the past lying under your heels,
Wash the ruined temples with your tears!
We live for a different beauty, we are free, we are brave.

The muscles of our arms long for a gigantic work,
With a creative pain the collective bosom burns,
With a wonderful honey we shall fill the combs,
For our planet we shall find a different, a glittering road.

We love life, and its intoxicating boisterous ecstasy,
Our spirit is tempered with a terrible struggle and agony.
We are all, we are in all, we are the conquering fire and light,
We are to ourselves God, Judge, and Law.

OCTOBER 25

There are days more stately than centuries:
Sparkle my song, and burn!
The autumn day is illumined
By the light of an immortal dawn.

Like puny beggars tottered the days
And disappeared in fog and mist;
This day has risen over the ancient graves
Like a groom beside his bride—the earth.

Posterity will never forget
Turbulent Smolny[2] with its buzzing hives,
The flames of words and its bonfires of guards
That pierced through fear and dark.

Everyone was a head taller,
Everyone was brave and strong.
I believe: even the constellations hear
These days' passionate song.

All were drunk, without vodka were intoxicated,
From dawn to dawn all were wide awake;
Something new was in every gait
And fire and spring in every gaze.

---

[2] Formerly a famous school for girls. During the Bolshevik revolution Smolny became the headquarters of the Bolshevik party.

KLUYEV, NIKOLAY ALEXEYEVICH

(b. 1887)

Kluyev was born of a peasant family. His father came from the Oka River valley, and his mother from the province of Vologda. All his childhood years were saturated with the poetry of folk songs, tales, and legends which were narrated to him by his mother. It was she who taught him to read and write. Later he traveled all over Russia.

He first became known as a poet in 1912, when a volume of his verse was published. Up to date his works number a dozen volumes.

THERE IS A VAST COUNTRY

There is a vast country upon the earth,
There grow the pine trees and the firs;
It is desolate, and it is unknown,
And it is the cradle of Russia's woe.

In this country of sadness and grief
There stands a prison all forsaken:
Like a rock amid the smooth seas
It is immobile and silent.

Beyond the ramparts tall,
The gray granite walls,
In a tower, like a caged bird,
A lonely maid is barred.

Bound by a wicked doom,
There she lingers and for freedom yearns,
There she waits from dawn till dawn,
From morn till night, from year to year.

But strong are the bolts at the doors,
Inaccessible are the threatening vaults,
And the echo from the vast wilderness
Rings not in the cells.

Only the tuneful breeze
Whispers to her from afar:
Cease thy cares, my princess dear,
Bright joy is already near.

Beyond the hazy dawn,
Clad in dazzling armor,
The long-awaited knight is speeding
Astride a frothing steed.

THERE ARE THE BITTER LOAM

There are the bitter loam, and the land thick with humus;
The humble clay, and the rubble with sand,
The soggy silt, the verdure's nectar;
And the mottled ochre, the desert dweller.

There is Mother Earth, Life's Fount,
Amidst the rich, the deep, the poor lands;
Her guardian is Fate, and her gardener is God:
To her, through life's dusk there leads no road.

Only her daughter—Fallow Land—in the harrowing season
Reveals, like a scroll, Destiny's decrees;
The tiller reads them, and so does Someone else with him:
'Tis he who rules o'er the fire and the soul of the peasant.

We are fire's kin, the grandchildren of the earth,
We enjoy the dawns and the taper's light;
The iron hurts us, so does the sooty shirt,
But our memory retains only the hues of bright rainbows.

Yearning for wings, we call
Handsome folk—''pea-hens'' or ''bright falcons.''
And mark ye now: the weathercock upon the roof
Is a silent proof of our distant journey.

The hut is a chariot, the corners are the wheels,
The seraphs will alight from the cloudy spheres.
Peasant Russia, in a great procession,
Will float aloft to meet the challenging storms.

The nations will vanish, the oceans will be drained,
With silks the sunrise will be embroidered;
'Tis our maidens, commemorating past ages,
Who spread their kerchiefs upon fairy plains.

THE RED SONG

Spread out, eagle's wings!
Toll, tocsin, and ye thunders rumble!
The fetters of oppression are now but broken links
And the prison of life has crumbled!
Vast are the Black Sea plains,
Turbulent is the Volga, and rich with gold the Ural;
Go, vanish into air, bloody block and chains,
Casemate and iniquitous tribunal!

> For land and freedom, for earned bread
> We march in arms to meet our foes!
> Upon us enough they did tread!
> Rush on to fight, to blows!

Over Russia there passed a fiery pheasant,
Kindling vehement wrath in the heart:
Virgin Mother—our little earth Thou art—
Bear Thou free bread for the peasant!
The rumors of old and the dreams have come true;
Svyatogor is the people, and now wide awake,
Honey is on the loaves of a rustic cake,
And the tablecloth shows a bright pattern too.

> For land and freedom, for earned bread
> We march in arms to meet our foes!
> Upon us enough they did tread!
> Rush on to fight, to blows!

Bread and salt, men from Kostroma and Volynia,
Olonets, Moskva, and Siberia!
Our freedom—the Lord's grace—
Is a bright beacon for the human race!
From Baikal to Crimea's warm clime
Will the ocean of waving rye float . . . .
Surpassing the stole of the seraph sublime
Sparkles the scarlet of Svyatogor's coat,

For land and freedom, for earned bread
We march in arms to meet our foes!
Upon us enough they did tread!
Rush on to fight, to blows!

To the peasant's Saviour ye offer a taper—
Knowledge his brother, and science his sister—
His face is of wheat, and his beard is a sunbeam,
Goodness and love are incarnate in him!
The Redeemer's eye is wearied of dusk,
And the golden calf is much hated;
Keatege-grad, the incense of pines of Sarovsk—
'Tis our own, the paradise we have awaited.

For land and freedom, for earned bread
We march in arms to meet our foes!
Upon us enough they did tread!
Rush on to fight, to blows!

Trust ye brothers, after hail and snow
The sunshine comes—our Lord's window;
Holy Grail brimming with blood—the world's sacrament—
We'll drink to the bottom—thus our destiny meant.

For land and freedom, for earned bread
We march in arms to meet our foes!
Upon us enough they did tread!
Rush on to fight, to blows!

KLYCHKOV, SERGEY ANTONOVICH

(b. 1889)

A native of the province of Tver, Klychkov belongs to a peasant family.

His first work, the short story "Tsar-Vanka" appeared in print in 1909, in the *Messenger of Self-Education*. Seven volumes of his verse were published during 1911 to 1923.

> The wilderness of native plain,
> The vernal murmur of the groves,
> And the cries of the cranes
> To me are dearer than any fame.
> There is no more wonderful mystery,
> There is no other beauty
> Than to scatter the grains of song
> O'er the virgin soil in spring!
> O my forest, meadow, field,
> Let it be so all my life!
> Let the callouses stay on my hand,
> And with my quiet song stay, O grief!

MALASHKIN SERGYEY IVANOVICH

(b. 1890)

Malashkin was born in Homyakovo, a village in the province of Tula, of a poor peasant family. He attended the rural parish school for a year. In 1904 he came to Moscow and worked for five years at a distillery. Since 1906 he has been a member of the Social Democratic party.

His first writings appeared in print in 1916, in a newspaper at Nizhni-Novgorod. Two volumes of his verse were published in 1919 and 1920.

THE BAND PLAYS

The band plays. The drums beat.
The trumpets triumphantly blare.
The boisterous tocsin is raging—
Its brass is inviting
And calling.
The band plays. The drums beat.
The trumpets triumphantly blare.

Countless masses, stormy and courageous,
Raising high the crimson banner toward the azure,
Scorning and forgetting the grief of ages—
From dawn to dawn,
With one mighty impulse,
They slowly pace,

Their resounding calls reverberating
In the streets and alleys of the Centre:
"Friends, toward the zenith, forward!
Sing! Let the song peal and thunder!"

> The band plays. The drums beat.
> The trumpets triumphantly blare.
> The boisterous tocsin is raging—
> Its brass is inviting
> And calling.
> The band plays. The drums beat.
> The trumpets triumphantly blare.

To the tribune the masses come nearer,
From their noisy stampede the city of concrete
Quivers with its steel wires that reach the distance;
In the aqueducts it loudly sings, in the iron pipes it hums;
It sings to the world, simply and crudely, like Homer,
Plunging itself into rapture.
The houses shout. The doors and windows are open.
Clad in bright wedding garments,
Veiled with the beams of a burning, ardent sun,
The new brothers meet them in friendship;
The new sisters with red crimson ribbons
Across their shoulders
Lovingly welcome them.
Keeping step, shoulder to shoulder,
With songs and hymns, themselves fervently praising,
And the turbulence of winged masses,
In love with the sun
They encircle the Centre.

> The band plays. The drums beat.
> The trumpets triumphantly blare.
> The boisterous tocsin is raging—
> Its brass is inviting
> And calling.
> The band plays. The drums beat.
> The trumpets triumphantly blare.

The masses are on the square. The festival, the tumult, the joy!
The beloved brothers and sisters in their meeting rejoice,
Forgetting factories, hammers, and chisels, and their torment,
Boldly they have taken one another's hands,
Knowing well that they all are friends:
They closely encircle the tribune,
Proclaiming brotherhood, the Commune,
As their indissoluble, reciprocal union;
And, with the ringing tocsin,
The summoning brass, they celebrate;
Turbulently, joyfully they await
Lenin, dearer to them than a brother,
With the sun of their eyes they smile;
From the tribune he will tell them,
In the words of the Messiah,
Of Communism in Soviet Russia
And of the universal victory of the proletariat.

> The band plays. The drums beat.
> The trumpets triumphantly blare.
> The boisterous tocsin is raging—
> Its brass is inviting
> And calling.
> The band plays. The drums beat.
> The trumpets triumphantly blare.

MAYAKOVSKY, VLADIMIR VLADIMIROVICH

(b. 1894)

The son of a forester in the province of Kutaiss, Maya-kovsky received his secondary education at a gymnasium. In 1906 he came to Moscow with the intention of continuing his studies. Two years later he became a member of the Social Democratic party, and worked as a propagandist. During this activity he was twice arrested. While serving his term in prison he turned to self-education and read a great deal. Later Mayakovsky entered the art school, where he met the famous futurist painter, Burlyuk, whom he regards as his "best friend" and his "real teacher" in the art of poetic expression.

His works began to appear in print in 1913. There are several volumes of his plays, satirical verse, and short stories.

THE LEFT MARCH

Turn about and march!
There is no room for bickering!
Quiet, ye orators!
Your turn,
Comrade Mauser!
We shall no longer abide
By the old laws of Adam and Eve,
The jade of history to death we will drive.

Left, left, left!
Rush ye,
Blue-bloused men,
Beyond the ocean!
Or did the men of war
In the roadstead make their sharp keels dull?
Let the British roar and grin beneath their crown,
And raise a howl.
The Commune shall not be cowed.
Left, left, left!
There
Beyond the sorrow's mounts
Is the sunny virgin land.
Make your millionth pace,
To do away with hunger,
To drain the oceans of plague.
Let them surround with mercenaries' band
And pour forth the steel lava—
Russia will not yield to the Entente.
Left, left, left!
Is the eagle's eye dimmed?
Shall we stare into the past?
Grip fast
On the world's throat
The proletariat's fingers!
Forward, with a bold heart!
With flags cloud the sky!
Who is marching with the right?
Left, left, left!

MOROZOV, IVAN IGNATIEVICH

(b. 1885)

Morozov comes from the province of Ryazan. At the age of two he lost his father. His mother taught him to read church Slavic. Later he attended the rural school, where the Russian classics, above all, Pushkin, made a great impression upon the child. While still at school Morozov made his first attempt at writing. In 1903 he came to Moscow where he was introduced to the Surikov literary circle. Two years later he served in the army, in the Far East.

His poems are to be found in many magazines. Three volumes of his verse were published during 1914 to 1919.

I CAME TO YOU

I came to you from Ryazan's lands
At your brotherly call, your friendly call;
I have brought with me legends and songs
Of my native Oka River banks.

I have come to you, bathing in dew,
Diving into the feather-grass sea,
And my faithful staff has disturbed
The corn-crake's evening chirp.

The smoke from the corn-kiln
Upon my head and shoulders still clings;
And the forefathers' speech, the ancient accents
Twist my uttered words.

My red shirt is bright,
The bast shoes are light,
The petals of fragrant clover
Still hang on the skirt of my coat . . . .

I have come to you from the levees,
To the festival of golden freedom I have come;
My humble songs for you have I brought,
And they glow with my heart's warmth.

Here in the throes of rapture
Let us closer fill our ranks,
That the black earth and the flowers
With stone and metal may unite.

RUS

My native land, my wooded plains,
Wide fields and lofty mountains!
A mighty hand cannot hold thee,
A proud gaze cannot take thee in!

The stalwart giants
Prop their heads against the skies,
They are stately and quiet—
Those sacred woods;

The silky rye ripens in peace,
Turbulently surge the seas . . . .
O, my beautiful Rus, thou hast
The spirit and might of a giant!

But will the uninvited guest
Thy spirit and thy temper guess
By thy wind-swept field,
Or by thine age-long grief?

When by disasters thou art driven
And covered with dust and patches,
In thee, O my own, I discern
The treasure ships.

I behold thee downtrodden,
But in thee I honor ever
Thy passion, thy latent vigor,
And thy dream's fiery ardor;

Thy vast plain, like a flooding stream;
Thy mighty daring—
This free song is for thee,
This pure song for thee I sing.

I sing and ever trust
In thy firm might:
Under thy gray dowlas shirt
A turbulent force abides.

She fears not black fate,
Nor for heat or cold does she care;
Is it not she that, persevering in labor,
Heaves mountains with her shoulders?

She bursts into a song—the whole universe trembles;
Grief is gone,
And faith in the sunny world
In the native tunes is heard.

O thou stalwart beauty,
O thou limitless plain!
The living Rus, the people's Rus,
Art thou not a titan?

II

For thee I yearn,
For thee I long;
Thy sadness to my heart is known,
And akin to me is thy boisterous song.

From early days to the setting years
Thou art mine, and I am thine;
To me thou art sacred and dear
Even in this grievous life:

In every poor hamlet,
On every scanty field,
In the huts of logs,
And in the beauty lost.

With thee I either weep,
Or artlessly play,
I am in raptures and say my prayers,
Or o'er my failures I grieve.

On my solitary road
With thy scanty good I am fed.
Rus of mine, I am thy beggar,
Give me thy shelter and warmth!

NECHAYEV, GEORGI EFIMOVICH

(b. 1859)

The son of a glazier, Nechayev is a native of the province of Tver. When the boy was nine years old he helped his father in the glass-house, where he had to work eighteen or twenty hours at a stretch. At about this time he began studying, paying fifty copecks a month for his lessons. But the factory work prevented his further education and the lessons lasted not more than three months. Not till at the age of seventeen was he able to resume his studying. At about this time he began to write. In 1885 he came to Moscow and was introduced into the Surikov literary circle.

His first verse appeared in print in 1891, and five volumes of his works were published during 1911 to 1922.

FREEDOM

The poison of insult and the bile of torment
Oppressed our souls like lead.
Raising our arms toward the skies
Our grievous bondage we cursed.

We have waited. There will rise the dawn,
And disperse the darkness of our native land.
And we shall be happier and warm
In the rainbow-tinted glitter of spring.

We waited, too long we waited
Under the yoke of darkness and dread;
We prayed, complained, and wept
And froze in winter's cold.

And then what? Of a sudden, like a magic dream,
A dream of May flowers,
Came to us with healing power
Dazzlingly beautiful Freedom.

Young, clad in gold,
With a wreath of lilies and roses;
With love, ineffable caresses,
And with a palm of peace in her hand.

Darkness is gone, the distance shines,
And boundless space is open,
Sadness and grief are forgotten,
And hearts and souls rejoice.

OBRADOVICH, SERGYEY ALEXANDROVICH

(b. 1892)

A native of the suburb of Moscow, Obradovich belongs to a family of artisans. He graduated with honors from the elementary school. At fifteen he began to work in a printing shop. Three years later he organized a self-educating circle among his fellow-workers. Thereafter he attended the University of Shanyavsky in Moscow. From 1914 to 1918 he took part in the war. Since the November revolution he has been a member of the Moscow *Proletkult,* and at present he is the secretary of the *Kuznitza* group.

Obradovich began writing at the age of fifteen. In 1912 his first poems were printed in the workers' magazine *Echo.* Since then he has brought out some ten volumes of verse.

THE BLUE–BLOUSED WORKMEN

Thou Past! Roar with the granite of Paris,
London, New York, and Tokio!
At the stock exchange, sparkle with gold and silver,
Burn incense to gods and ikons.

On dark and wicked nights
Howl over our convulsions,
Pray for our peril with a wolf's howl,
For our peril, for our eternal rest!

Thou wilt not hear a despairing groan—
I know—like a dreadful defoliation;
In the parks and suburbs roam
Prostitutes and paupers.

I know: in the desolate fields,
Into the same furrows that he had ploughed,
The peasant, overburdened with the last bitter **grain**,
Tottering fell.

Life is an idle jade,
Life is not a spurred faithful steed;
But more unflagging grows the pace,
With bright fire gleam restless eyes.

Through prisons, chasms, and dreary days,
Trampling over darkness and pain
My cry of iron is today
For all who are not deaf or blind;

Whose hearts have not yet sunk
In mildew, tatters, and smoke;
For all with callouses and sores:
"Come out on the arena of revolt and song."

Forgetting prayers and books of Buddha,
Mohammed, Christ, and others,
All countries listen to the stormy tones,
To the songs, and the spasmodic groans.

There run over Europe's roads,
With fire-scorched eyelids open,
Milliard-mouthed Murmur,
And thundervoiced Revolt.

Hear ye! Journeymen of the world's plantations,
Factories, fields, quarries,
Blue-bloused men of all races and nations:
Destroy all strawlike weakness!

Today, workmen, the earth, all the earth,
Crimsoning on the streets and paths,
Discards the black blouse of night,
And echoing with our songs now rings . . . .

I know: our step is painful and full of torture,
Tottering and weak from starvation.
But the smoke-dimmed eye is watching,
And the heart is the charge of a gun.

THE FACTORY

For half a season, by stillness bound
And the coldness of concrete walls,
In deep anguish it stood dumb
Amid the rust of iron moulds.

In the fog of troublous days,
It hearkened, numb and abandoned,
How October with its wet soles
Wandered through public squares.

The days drag on with a shuffling pace
Over the vigilant ground.
The freezing zero has bound
The rigid dynamometer on the furnace.

Then only the midnight watchmen
Through the desolate place passed slowly.
And startled the silence of machines
With the beat of their rattles.

In winter the storm with snowballs
Pelted the barred doors
And tore Voencom's[3] order
Off the seamed brick walls . . . .

---

[3] Decree of the Secretary of War.

It stood there, stern and sunk in thoughts
Submissive to the times, dumb and deaf . . . .
And oft o'er the silent lathes
A spider wove his steely web.

II

At last on a day in spring
A hand removed the bolts,
And with a hiss, with frothing communicators,
The fly-wheel ran triumphantly its course.

For half a season tortured with plague and hunger,
It was faint and dead and—of a sudden
Motor after motor buzzed
With the beat of hearts and hands.

The fiery rails again are cut
With the teeth of saws here and there;
Here and there with gnashing and roar,
In sweat, in grime, they forge and forge.

The cast-iron beams tremble:
After each blow follows a stronger blow;
Of victory sing the saws,
O'er the furnace quickly throb the bellows.

Again it is full of ceaseless clangor
Amidst the sultry hum of the square,
And above the sighing concrete
There is the smiling day.

Freed by an ardent hand,
Burning infirm old age,
The factory rose on the earth
Triumphant and bright, like the sun.

ORESHIN, PYOTR VASILIEVICH

(b. 1887)

The son of a peasant from Saratov, Oreshin studied four years at the municipal school.

His literary activity began in 1913, when his first verse was printed in the St. Petersburg magazine *Zavety*. Since then about fourteen volumes of his works have appeared.

THE BAY NAG

Will our bay nag pull through?
Will he pull the loaded cart
Towards that happiness soaring into the blue
Of which we dreamt in our slumber?

We, all Russia's tillers,
Not for nothing are we harnessed to this cart.
Bluer than the days of spring
From the wet hair steam rises in clouds.

In every look there is bitterness and struggle;
And common pain and combat
And joy are like a heavy weight
Upon Russian shoulders wet with sweat.

Will our dear one pull through?
The dawn is near—just one step more.
I believe: e'en the world's load
For the rye shoulders is not too strong.

We shall not be left out in the cold.
No heaven for us, only give us land!
We should be glad to behold
Conflagrations where once we stood.

The nag's legs bend,
He snorts, his nostrils are aflame;
His hide is torn on the way,
Like a crimson dawn is his long neck . . . .

Will the bay nag pull through?
It is all the same to me.
The world's nag, I am proud of thee,
Of thee—Rus, who all the world didst move.

THE CRIMSON TEMPLE

Through the scorched wheaten waves
I bring from the sun the Crimson Temple:
Liberty to cots and hamlets,
Liberty to beggars and slaves.

Is it not Rus that is ablaze,
Is it not Rus that is crimson to the bottom?
Is it not Rus that amid the tocsin's laughter
With the fiery glare is lighted all over?

The dowlas coat is of flame and gilt,
The perfume spreads over droning fields;
Under the glowing standard
There burns the Russian land.

For dreams there is no room in my bosom,
My soul is on wings of gold.
Holy Russia is my bride
And I am her beloved groom.

Away with sorrow's frown!
Now I am joyous and bold:
Over the abysses, the chasms and waterfalls
The Angel of Freedom has flown.

Over each hut, the bird of gladness!
Over each hut, the fiery dream!
And the wind kisses the red lips
Of the night's pale face.

The roads 'mong thickets are bright,
The tapers flare on the hills,
The Crimson Temple of Free Citizens
Is all ablaze with sunlight.

THE SAVIOUR

Open wide all shutters and doors;
The new hour is striking.
In the cellars there walks
The ancient miraculous Saviour.
Peace be with ye, brethren, give shelter tonight
To the eternal wanderer;
I am no trader, neither king nor noble knight,
But only—a man!
We have sheltered him. He calls one a brother,
We who are tainted with sin are loved
By the miraculous Redeemer
That is crucified on a cross of silver.

KVASS

I know the murmur of the ringing
Corn that ripens in its sleep,
The fragrant rye's greetings
To my native country.

I know the curves of roads,
I have lived through the sultry days of harvest;
I love the golden straw
On the roofs of Russian hamlets.

I love the aftermath of green,
The rows of sickles and the blade's sheen.
The rustling whirl of the vagabond wind
Amidst the silvery birch-trees.

I love the cheerful peasant's laughter
Upon the dark rustic face;
And the ancient customs of my forefathers,
And the meetings at dusk on the steps.

I love it all—for into these huts soon
There will come the new day.
And the silver-haired yesterday
Will be reaped and mown.

I love to wake in the early morn,
When all the sky is aflame with dawn.
By the rosy wind-flowers I glide
Sinking into the morning rye.

With the clanging scythes the waves fall,
The curly sheaves are on the thrashing floor,
And on a hot noon
A draft of peasant kvass is good.

O native country mine, how beautiful thou art:
The steppes of rye, the people of rye,
The rye sun, and in thy songs
There sing the earth and the rye.

POMORSKY, ALEXANDRE NIKOLAEVICH
(b. 1891)

Pomorsky was born in a village on the river Volkhov, near St. Petersburg. His parents moved to the capital, where the boy received his secondary education. While still attending school he had to earn his living in a factory. As a common workman he for the first time caught a glimpse of the socialist movement. In 1908 he became a member of the Social Democratic party. During the years 1913 to 1917 he was often arrested and imprisoned.

In 1912 Pomorsky began to write in the Social Democratic newspapers *Zvezda* ("The Star") and *Pravda* ("The Truth"). There are three volumes of his works, consisting of verse and dramatic pieces.

THE FLOWERS OF REVOLT

Into your hearts we will throw the flowers of revolt!
We will not kneel in prayers,
We have no mercy for priest or god,
We who are enlightened by the great combat.

The flowers of revolt will set the world astir,
And moments into eternity will turn;
The flowers of revolt will awaken the strings of the lyre;
Breathing into them inspiration and life.

And, like the tocsin of future beauty,
In the purple flames of turbulent revolt
They will strew the rainbow flowers
Of Renascence and Liberty.

TO THE CITY

A monster, with eyes afire,
A sleepless dragon of iron and stone . . . .
You have clutched us with an iron vise,
Into a dreadful howl you have turned our groan.

With a bright hope and azure dreams
You lure us from fields, woods, and vale;
Stooping at the lathes, with a feverish look,
We listen to your ardent tale.

We listen to you, but we ourselves—we build the dams,
In the harbor we prop the fallen poles . . . .
To your own self you sing your dithyrambs,
And shout at us that we are your slaves.

Yes, your slaves we are. We are born slaves.
But every stone of yours is our warm sweat.
The struggle calls. In its great temple
Your dissolute brawl is ridiculous, insipid . . . .

Be quiet, you tyrant crowned by fools,
A dragon with a mutilated face!
You will be ours. Before the unhappy slaves
You yourself will fall, a humiliated slave!

THE WORKMAN'S PALACE

On the dark tombs of the rubbish of the past,
Of the laughter and tears of our worn hearts—
We, full of pride, build; we, full of pride, build:
We build the workmen's palace.

Our vigor stirs us. Our hands are strong.
We know how to build, though dark is the night;
And stone upon stone, stone upon stone,
Wall after wall arises.

Above us the frowning sky is overcast—
Many a man in our ranks falls exhausted.
We, full of pride, build; we full of pride, build:
We build the workmen's palace . . . .

It will rise in the mist of silent nights;
It will pierce, like the sun, the mirage of fate;
An iron host, we shall arrive, we shall arrive:
Without tears, without chains, not like slaves!

More courage, comrade, fear not the nightmare!
Follow us, whoever you are!
And, if you believe, if you believe in the new era,
Lay the foundation stone . . . .

On the dark tombs of the ruins of the past,
Of the blood and tears of our worn hearts,
We, full of pride, build; we, full of pride, build:
We build the workmen's palace.

PRASKUNIN, MICHAIL VASILIEVICH
(b. 1877)

Praskunin comes of a peasant family from the province of Ryazan. He attended the rural parish school. Later he worked at the iron works in Kolomna. In 1909 he came to Moscow.

His first writings appeared in print in 1904, in Harbin. Three volumes of his verse were published during 1912 to 1918.

THE TILLER

Tossing rythmically the bridle of bast,
The battered jade paces the furrows.
The tiller pressed his bosom
To the ancient plough: under the tattered dowlas
For sighs there is no room.

Since childhood the wretch is used to toil,
With force the peasant bends his knees;
His help the bay jade needs.
With a whisper the humble tiller
Treads the black scorched soil.

The sun kisses and fondles the fields,
The tiller's bast shoes with earth are filled;
His cap slides down over one ear,
Not for nothing the dark loaf of rye is given
To the poor wretch.

The sounds in the air ring in chorus,
There is no time to gaze upon the heaven;
Yonder the guilt is not for us,
The furrowed fields for every span
The peasant's blood and sweat demand.

RADIMOV, PAVEL ALEXANDROVICH

(b. 1887)

Radimov is the son of a peasant. His verse first appeared in print in 1912. Five volumes of his works have been published.

I SING OF THE FIELDS

I sing of the fields drunk with vernal sun,
Of the cranes crying in the skies,
Of the golden sun glittering in the stream,
Of the green reeds bathed in the river.

I sing that there is much joy in life,
Such an intoxicating wilderness in the green fields!
I know my heart: in it a longing is born
For the playful sun, for the unknown worlds.
This longing with the cry of the cranes is born.

SADOFIEV, ILYA IVANOVICH

(b. 1889)

Sadofiev was born in St. Petersburg, where his father, a peasant, was then employed in a factory. From the age of six to thirteen the boy lived with his parents in a village, where he attended school. Subsequently he returned to St. Petersburg, where he earned his living first as a waiter, then as a factory worker. After 1905 he studied in a night school. In 1916 he was sentenced to six years of exile for membership in the Social Democratic party. He was released after the March revolution of 1917.

He began writing at the age of ten. His work first appeared in print in 1913. Since then he has published four volumes of prose and verse.

THE MORNING PRAYER

At dawn, the silent wistful hour,
In suburbs of the cities—giants,
Waking, calling the multifaced Creator;
Ringing, the cadence streams forth,
The masterful voice of excited,
Threatening, boisterous and boiling steam:
The voice is a fused singing, a well-tuned chorus,
Of the triumphant factory whistles.

Soaring, floating, it beats upon the breasts of the masses' legions,
Tearing apart the giddy veil of dreams,
Into proud and open hearts it pours vigor;
Far and wide and high it floats,
Betokening to the oppressed millions
Revolts, victories, and broken fetters,
Welcoming with an ardent hymn the blazing sun
Of the New and Happy Age.

> The night is pale,
> The darkness is thin,
> The light breaks in,
> Listen! .... A prayer,
> A call to Fight,
> A hymn to Labor!
> I am awake,
> I dress;
> Steps echo,
> Uproar, the gates,
> To work
> I go.

There is nothing more appealing, masterful,
Clear, ardent, and tuneful,
More inspiring and beautiful
And triumphant and free,
Than the early morning prayer of the fused and tuneful chorus
Of the factory whistles, calling to fight, startling the night.

Trembling and listening to this song,
A village song I have recalled:
Monotonous and dreamy tunes
Of bells ringing hymns—
To a god of idleness, revenge, and anger,
Of evil, submission, humbleness,
Senile, white with age like chalk, and deaf,
On the seventh day retiring for his eternal rest.

Trembling and listening to this song
I comprehend the wisdom of the world.
The choir of whistles—the universal tongue,
The hymn of Unity, the hymn of Labor,
The awakening of imprisoned Thought,
The wires from heart to heart.
To the Man god rises this song, to the Victor, the Fighter,
To the indefatigable Creator, the titan artist . . . .

AT THE LATHE

The shavings curl, the shavings stretch and creep,
Growing long like parting, like grief.
But the chisel runs; it laughs and sings,
It kisses, and it strips the virgin steel.
The pinions, the sheaves rotate and gleam.
With the dance of wheels
Two desires in my bosom, two great principles dispute.
In the soft murmur of belts a voice I hear:
"O poet, free-thinker, O dreamer!
Wert thou born into the world
To suffer torments in the factory all thy life
That chained to the machines thou shouldst die?
There is spring outside thy window . . . . beauty . . . . glittering sun.
Here the eye is dimmed with filth and gloom,
There a chorus of feathered singers caresses the ear,
Here the monster machines babble and boom;
It is the reproach, the fathers' curse:
Sinking in the roar, sob the grating chisels.
Over there is the fragrance of flowers, the trees;
Here—always smoke, and stench, iron, steel.
Here—everything whirls, trembles, bounces,
Howls, clangs, roars, drones, and pounds.
Thou art always at the lathe in the workroom;
The mind is dull . . . . The back aches . . . . The chest is sore . . . .
And see how kindly the sun looks,

How tenderly he kisses, how much joy he pours forth;
He teases, lures, and persistently calls;
"To the open boundless plains, to freedom,
To the green and flowery carpet;
To the resounding sea and the playful surf,
To the mountains! Higher . . . .
Nearer to the sun! To the skies!" . . . .

. . . .

Enchanted with the chorus of sounds, convinced,
I curse the factory's prison, the clang of steel;
Toward the sun, sea, hills, toward freedom I flee.
Bright happiness and joy I desire.
Is it not true that the road to pleasure is open
To the oppressors who are doing no work?
To those who grow fat all is granted, all is given!
What am I destined for but torment?
Or the machine guns in the foundry shall I forge?
"What are they for?"—my son will ask. What shall I tell him?
How can I say, "The grapes will ripen in them,
And perhaps with them you will be fed?"
The heart pounds, anger bubbles, wrath seethes . . . .
In my ears the ringing call does not cease:
"You see, you—slave and pariah, what a glitter . . . .
And in the factory at the machine you linger . . . . "

. . . .

Thus did I dream, toward the heights I rose, I soared.
I did not see who stopped the lathe.
A shout . . . . The foreman . . . . Again I switch the commutator . . . .
The stately dance of sounds again.
Now predicting, singing of different things
With a steely voice, a bold masterful tongue:
"Disperse the tipsy chorus of your dreams,
Curse not the factory, the lathes and the machines!
Hither you came from the sunny vale,
Where, under the henchman's yoke, you were a slave;
Here you curse the metal that calls to fight,

There you groaned under your master's whip.
Here the belts tell you of the sun,
There, suffering, you were not glad to see the light.
Hence! Your ancestor calls you back to plains and hills!
There—under a cart you slept in the fields;
There—you wandered humble and alone;
Here—the factory has united you all in one!
There—you pined in long and dreadful anguish,
Here—the talk, the beat of the machines calls you to Freedom!
There—the priest dazed you with a false creed,
Here—the factory has set all your reason free:
It pours into your breast Vigor, Faith, Protest, Wrath,
And leads you out upon the pure and fiery road!
Here the meaning of Life, the aim of Life is made clear to you.
Here is the fount of all striving and revolt!
Only listen and understand the talk of the machines:
'You are the future Master, you are the Messiah . . . .
With steam, steel, and fire you are allied;
You will capture the globe—the spherical boat;
You will conquer the black foe,
And, acquitted and bathed, the world
Will be young again.' . . . . ''
Like a clock's pendulum did I vacillate
Between the two voices and the different calls;
In the first—something tender echoed in my heart;
In the other—the victorious Principle of Labor!
Two roads before me branched:
To go toward the past, or toward the future . . . .
I hesitated, for many days could not decide,
I wondered which one was more happy and bright.
And having thought it over—I took
The second, the road toward the future . . . .
Thus I went toward Struggle, Freedom, into the distance, forward!
I loved then the factory—the fount of all striving.

THE FLUTE OF INDUSTRY

(*A Poem*)

PROLOGUE

O thou elemental force, my soul's mistress,
The lightning arrow of my thought!
To thee I sing my resonant verse,
For thee is my ardent heart's blood.

Once thou didst call me
To thy furnaces, away from my fir trees.
And with this fiery lust
We both, like the sunshine, burn.

When to the silk hats and coupons
Thou wert a slave and odalisque,
With an iron clang thou didst sing to me:
"O rescue me, my dear, my own;

"Into my arms, my sweetheart,
Come, to thee I shall not lie!"
And as if it were heaven's door
I touched thy burning mouth,

And passion surged like a tide . . . .
We knew: without love we should die! . . . .
The creative passion soon made thee mother,—
Thou wert delivered of a child—October.

To the cannon's rumble,
Swinging the cradle
In a reverberating chorus,
To a creative love thy flute again calls.

To me thou art now still dearer,
Still more longed-for, my own!
I swear by the love of our youth,
By the love of the Future days;

I shall not cease to kiss thee,
My mistress and mother,
Dynamo-Industry!
I shall not cease to sing to thee,
My mistress and mother,
This melodious liturgy!

O SEDITIOUS, FIERY, PASSIONATE FACTORY

O seditious, fiery, passionate factory,
O thou who hast reared me!
For many years thou didst stoop my back,
And together we went to the executioner's rack.

We both were prisoners
In a festered stream of long years,
And thy volcanic womb
Devoured the heavy trail of woe . . . .

Crucified upon thine iron bars
I cursed: "the city-octopus,"
And wicked, slavish labor,
By eternal serfdom branded.

To the son of pines and heather
Thine iron embraces
Were the Lord's curses
And the devil's powerful fetters.

Was it not thou who every day
Called the slaves, your victims, with a shrill "I wait"?
Only in the angry February blast
Didst thou shatter the bridle of the arbitrary past.

A turbulent stream of flowery words,
Thou didst flow to October,
When brighter than the scarlet tints
The Universal Dawn was kindled.

Burying in tombs the past.
The Soviet citizen can see
In this cosmic avalanche
The factory's creative force.

In thy triumphant rumble
Prayers and psalms are drowned . . . .
Not to believe in miracles hast thou taught us,
But to create happiness upon the earth.

Oppressions wolfish snout October slapped
With a fence of factory stacks,
And proud, freed Labor
To Victory was betrothed.

CALLING TO UNITED WORK

Calling to united work, the factory whistles
Had startled the owl, doubt.
Again the life-giving fount
Is frothy, and afresh it seethes.

Again in the suburbs the living stream
Of creative hosts blusters:
We will file, saw, forge, and plane
The hunchback of chaos, the ribs of fate.

The communicators sing again,
Upon the rails slides the weighty crane;
From the forges come thunder and uproar,
From the boilers a shrill tempest rolls.

Factory life bubbles like a stream;
One pressure of a callous hand,
And the sharp chisel will tap
The cankers of the sterile fields.

About the throats of sooty stacks
Death circled like an evil bird of prey;
The factory with a triumphant stroke
Burned his bony frame at the stake.

Now the infidel whispers not
That the keys to life he cannot find;
The foundries, like volcanoes,
Burn the gray sorrow and woes.

The factory leads to the red carnival,
Through its fiery gates,
Those who in the Commune do not believe,
Who prayed for our peril!

There, happiness will last for ever,
And the factory—turbulent, ardent—
With the galaxy of its cupolas
Will kindle the flames of the future.

And the lifeless hand
Will never still
The moving factory fly-wheel
Christened in the bloody stream.

WITH WHAT JOY THROBS

With what joy throbs
The factory's fiery heart,
When they open the gates
To fellow-believers, their comrades.

With what stirring accord
Of whistles the orchestra burst forth.
The eyes of doubt and sorrow
Were kindled with rapture's sunny glow.

What a gruesome tale,
What pages of base revenge upon foes
The smoky suburbs unveiled
To the home-coming heroes.

The past, the bloodthirsty tiger,
Was wont
To pursue freedom, bought with blood,
As if it were his prey.

The serfs of the tawny lioness, Europe,
Filling their pockets with gold,
Threw gloomy oppression's noose
Over the sad factory's throat.

Bouquets of flattery—and treason—
To the laborer's rainbow freedom;
In the city the aqueducts, in Moscow,
The treacherous exploding blasts.

The henchmen's daggers pierced
The tortured back and bosom;
Blood flowed from the wound,
And bondage, like a barn owl, screeched.

And oft on a dark night one dreamt
Of tortures and the knouts of old.
It seemed—the Calvary of the oppressing ages
Would reign again.

Then in militant triumph
The sufferings and nightmares were burnt,
And the communards
Their sunny tale have begun.

THE EARTH CALLS

The earth calls to the spring sowing,
Glittering ecstasy rings,
In the universe there will sparkle soon
Fulfillment's sunny zenith.

In harmonious, joyous accord
The booming factory roars;
The legions in overalls
March toward it, throng upon throng.

The soul, stirred with the sounds,
Like a red carnation blossomed,
To the lathes and foundries—the seeds and grain—
The envoys from the village came.

Of their empty fields,
Of their scarred backs,
Of ploughs and scythes they spake—
And this complaint was like the July heat.

The factory's equal, and its devotee,
The warrior of class victory,
Gives them with brotherly love
The nosegay of undying hope.

'Tis the response of the factory martyr,
The victor in strife,
The lathes clang, and the motors drone,
And the whistles sing together.

In all the furnaces soon
The sacrificial fire will burn;
Under a heavy load in the fields
The bright-eyed iron steed will neigh.

And many others, tens and hundreds
Upon resounding rails will pound.
Thus in peaceful labor the factories will heal
The cankers of the fields.

In a single feat of labor
The factory will melt disaster's load,
Blessing with an ardent love
The union of sickle and hammer.

IN THE FACTORY

Only today I have felt, only today I have comprehended,
Here, in the factory, the daily, noisy festive carnival.

Daily, at an appointed hour, the steam sings out inviting.
The guests are gaily clad, there are peals and roars, dancing and
       singing.
The peals and cadence of ringing uproar—the speech of sounds
       without words.
The shapely rhythmical dance of sheaves—joyful and drunken.

In the dance there is the dream of youth, eternal motion, and
       freedom.
In the sounds is the world's secret, in the sounds are the words
       of wisdom.
In the songs are vigor, inspiration, burning faith, challenge, and
       anger.
Oh, how sweet it is to hear this tune so passionately ardent.

Men in overalls understand these words and cries . . . .
Men in overalls are like titans, stern and proud, and quiet.

In their silence there is a hidden wisdom, a strength, a creating
       force;
And in their movements—power of steel, sternness, will, might.

To understand the iron tongue, to hear the mystery of the revela-
       tion;
To learn from the machines and lathes the boisterous force—how
       to destroy,
And how to create incessantly something brand new and different;
To be in the factory daily, to be there, is ecstasy!

TO RUSSIA

O my beloved mother! the Soviets' mother!
O cradle of beautiful and happy ages!
An enchanted isle of freedom and light art thou,
A tocsin that cheers and summons the enslaved.

From the Asiatic shackles of Mongol khanates,
From the autocratic-tsarist servile chains,
From the passionate embraces of the commoners revolution
To the commune you came—the best days' incarnation.

Like a torch, like a guiding beacon you are glittering,
The sensitive hearts of the oppressed you stir . . . .
Brothers from abroad to revolt you spur,
To break the fiery and bloody ring.

Alone, always without help or relief,
Heroically you fight the tyrants of the world.
Almost dead from wounds, you are pressed by the foes,
As by a steel band of violence and deceit.

I hear how alarm knocks at your heart,
I see the marks of weariness on your brow:
But one step, one more step upon the chosen path,
The hour will strike—to crown you with victory's crown.

Let those beyond the border linger—the calm before the storm
        and thunder—
Listen and understand, the inevitable blast will follow!
Watch the sinuous lightning's arrow,
Look! There crawls the cloudy smoke of gunpowder.

With electricity the thick air is saturated,
And all the countries are a rumbling volcano.
I feel: the path will be cleared soon
For the brotherhood of the oppressed of all countries and races.

O mother of mine, I hear the Marseillaise hymn
And the distant cadence of steps:
I see the barricades; the countless moving masses;
The corpses of bankers and tsars; the broken fetters!

I see: the distance is red with flames;
'Tis milliards of crimson flags and banners afloat . . . .
Under them—triumphant, proud, bold,
Our international comrade, Proletariat, enters the world.

He rushes like an avalanche, master of the world,
To the universal feast, the joyful, brotherly repast:
The old world, with an odor of prayers, mothballs, and moss
Blinks at the sun like an owl.

The crystal and marble edifice rose to the clouds:
The all-powerful Soviet of the workmen . . . .
There—you are the favorite president of the meeting,
The earth, circling amid the planets, is proud of you.

I behold: all the earth is clad with flowers;
All breathe joy and creative endeavor;
Murders, hatred, and torments have ceased.
The earth is the abode of unity, brotherhood and ease.

I look upon you with my keen sight;
I am your son, brother, and husband, your soldier and bard;
I am your feelings and ideals, your fine hearing and sight:
You are in my heart—with millions of hearts.

I measure eternity with their united pulse,
I sense the flux of other times and epochs;
I conceive in the harmony of tender chords
Immortality, the universal union of tongues and races.

My beloved country! Though to death you bleed,
You do not curse the brothers late for your succor;
You—the proletarian heart—you know, you feel,
He will arise whom you await—the master of the world.

My country, keep up your courage! The last moments
Of the impartial, punctual hours vanish in the past.
After them the universal revolution and movement,
Victory and freedom will solemnly pass.

One more effort of the cradle of the commune,
And the sun of new life will shine upon earth!
The tottering camarilla of the world you will meet
With revolt—that is your inherent duty.

SAMOBYTNIK (pseudonym)
(b. 1884)

Alexey Ivanovich Mashirov, a native of St. Petersburg, is the son of a craftsman. At the age of twelve he worked in a foundry. The year 1905 found him among the ranks of the Social Democratic party. During 1908–1909 he attended courses at the People's Institute. There he studied the history of literature and from time to time delivered lectures on the Russian classics.

His first writings were printed in 1913. So far he has published three volumes of verse.

THE WILL

One must be straight and stern,
And till the end be firm,
And, with a mighty word, like a fighter
One must inspire all hearts.

One must be a communard without fear;
The hour of battle draws near . . . .
Before the enemy's stroke
Do not avert your front.

One must know that without struggle
One cannot worst the dark forces of life,
One must know that perchance
One may fall in battle.

One must look into the distance without fear
Through the terrible years;
And, dying, devotedly believe
In the immortality of Labor.

THE REVOLUTION

You should have broken up the ice of dismal life
With a gigantic heavy mattock,
And raised the stern tillers' crop
With thunder and lightning.

You should lovingly have scattered the pearls
Of cheerful rain upon the earth.
But by timid and cowardly souls
You are treacherously betrayed.

With their helmets down,
Like ants they writhe in the battle,
With their heads bowed
They face proud capital.

With an ugly and heavy pall
They have covered you at dawn.
But again away you have flown
And the breath of spring is in October.

II

Was it you that to the menacing crags
The angry troops did rush?
Like the waves, the sailors dash about,
And thunders rumble from their armor.

The earth trembled with a victorious hymn,
Aurora proudly sent her shells:
The haughty Winter Palace fell
At the soldiers' and workmen's feet.

And into the face of your foes
The steely decrees you throw:
"I am living again, to the Soviets all the power!
In calloused hands is the power."

Let your spirit be young for ever,
Like the foaming surf of the ocean;
Over yonder on the Red Banner
The sickle and the hammer shine like the sun.

RUSSIA

My native country! In that terrible year,
Upon climes heated with blood
Thou didst flash in thy turn
Like a comet newborn.

At thy fiery baptizing
The silver bugles trill.
The huts in the fields
To the machines' roar are rising.

The Soviets' wrought-iron might
Shines proudly like the sun.
My country, to thunders wilt thou succumb
Under the yoke of wicked wrath?

Oh, no! Thy calling is to live
In Europe's mournful dusk,
To tread upon immortal paths
Toward brotherhood and love.

In vain the hostile elements
Are incited by the hatred of foes;
Amid the arctic snows
Ardent Russia flames.

TO THE REVOLT

Turbulent, like the boundless ocean,
I call to you in the fateful hour of combat;
Answer to my seditious call,
You—since childhood maimed in storm.

I am younger than you, but in the flames of conflagration
My spirit was tempered for new battles and wounds;
For the last terrible blow
Come, ye oppressed of all the world!

All the world burns in the embraces of iron,
And the new world—in the revolt of Labor.
Unite the fiery wires
Of your tempestuous thought, of all your power!

O, if your hammer made
The earthly globe quake daily,
Will you not have the wrathful strength
To break the servile chains?

Turbulent, like the boundless ocean,
I call to you, pressing my sword:
To revolt! Into your camp abroad
I throw my flaming wreath of wounds!

ON OUR POST

We are the stars in the gloomy dark,—
We burn with hardly a spark;
But from our lofty post
We faithfully guard.

At times our canopy we flood
With a sudden dazzling light,
Or with the first song freely sung
Into a dismal abyss we dash.

Fulfilling our secret pledge
We keep the fire all night,
All night our sky is kept warm
With the hope of a sunny morn.

It will come, we know,
The mighty sun will rise!
And we—relieved—we shall thaw
Amid our blue heights.

SANNIKOV, GRIGORI ALEXANDROVICH

(b. 1899)

Sannikov was born of an artisan family, in the province of Viatka. He attended a municipal school. In 1916 he came to Moscow and there joined the Social Democratic circle. He attended the University of Shanyavsky, but had to leave it because of his active service in the Red Army. During 1918 to 1920 he worked in the *Studio* of the Moscow *Proletkult* under the instruction of Andrei Bely. At present he is a member of the *Kuznitsa* group.

His first writings appeared in 1917. So far four volumes of his works have been published.

ON THAT NIGHT

To L. Trotsky

I knew a great iron cemetery—
On a forsaken lot beyond the city
The engines stood in black rows,
Bound with sleep.
In front of the deserted temple
A sooty depot dismally rose;
Leaving their work, extinguishing the forges,
To fight the workmen went.
Away they went . . . .
Long and empty the days dragged on;
There was no roar, no clangor of iron,
The hammers pounded not.
Only shrill and motley rain—

Long, long and persistent—poured down
On this great cemetery,
On this dead
But gloomy and menacing power.
And then, I do not remember
Whether it was a dream
Or whether this really happened.
It was a dark autumn night,
A thick heavy silence hung over the cemetery,
The engines stood dumb,
Their dark passions hiding;
Into the empty fields they stared
Paralyzed with iron fright.
Suddenly there was a whistle:
The alarm call over the dead
Hissed with despair,
Waking the iron sleep.
Like a beast howling in the dark of night,
Calling his lost mate.
Like a beast it growls—
No, not like a beast. Thus the martial bugler
His bugle blows
When the army starts its march.
To the trumpets' call, to the signal call
On the forsaken lot, all of a sudden
The dead rusty engines awakened.
Like black shadows they clutched
The startled night.
Piercing the silence with noise,
Filling it with iron motion,
They heavily sighed.
Throbbing in the cylinders
The mighty steam has struck the piston;
The regulators, by themselves, have opened.
Trampling the rails with an iron gait,
With groans and rumble,
And trumpets' blare
Piercing the dark,

The alert engines started
Like an iron host of stupendous order.
The earth shuddered,
The heavens grew higher and wider,
And the retreating moon threw light
Upon the engines' iron uprising.
On that night
The workmen entered the city.

HYMN OF THE TOMBS

Every night, when in the city
The noise ceases, and lights are out,
Under the Kremlin walls
The dead awaken in their tombs.
Their black rows rise from the gloom;
They enter the Kremlin in black rows:
On their alarmed faces is woe;
On their clothes, clotted blood.
Upon the ancient steps as of old,
Under the Kremlin's brick vaults,
To the steep tower they ascend
And in a circle noiselessly stand.
Their brass voices,
Stirring the quiet midnight,
As if upon a silent signal
Sing rhythmically the International.
And the words of the last fight
Of the awakened mankind
In a brass chord over the city drone,
And full of anguish they drown in the night,
Every night from the tower of the Kremlin
The hymn of the workman is heard.
'Tis the dead that of the fight are singing,
'Tis the dead that will rouse the living.

D. SEMENOVSKY

No biographical data available.

COMRADE

Like the breeze in spring, so new and sudden,
Among us passed the holy word,
The sacred word:
    "Comrade!"
Like a song for us it sings.
There is ardent faith, and hope and fervor,
The triumph of joy, and the storm of revolt,
And from brothers to brothers a greeting:
    "Comrade!"
There is no name more beautiful;
It is united with the red banner,
With the people's rapture, yearning and passionate,
And with the storm of its anger:
    "Comrade!"
For us brotherhood is the dearest of all.
We will forge happiness for our native land,
And like the wonderful Eden
Our free land will be
    "Comrade!"
We are force, we are one single will.

SHKULEV, FILIP STEPANOVICH

(b. 1866)

The son of a peasant from Pechatniki, a village in the province of Moscow, Shkulev was educated in an elementary school. At the age of twelve he began to earn a living in a factory. His further intellectual training consisted mainly in reading the classic Russian authors and socialistic pamphlets. In 1905 Shkulev became an active member of the Social Democratic party. He was arrested in 1911 and condemned to one year's solitary confinement. From 1913 to 1916 he wrote articles for many socialist periodicals. Shkulev's first verses appeared at the end of 1916. Several volumes of his poetry were published in Moscow, from 1918 to 1923.

THE REVOLUTION

Great is she, born in serfdom,
Amidst fetters, grief and oppression;
Amidst people whose life, like the night, is dark
From blood and tears, sweat and work.

She was fondled in languishing mines,
Within murky factory walls,
In the simple thoughts and ardent hearts
Of men driven by want.

She was christened with sword and blood,
With the torture of evil bondage and fire;
Pursued by the executioner, she did not die
Under the yoke of her hateful lot.

Beloved, radiant, she came
On the gloomy days of the people's tempest,
And swept away all curse and shame,
Soaring like a whirlwind into the heavens.

Victorious, into dust she turned all,
With her impertinent, masterful hand;
On the ashes and ruins of bonfires
She builds for us a new and beautiful world.

SMIRNOV-SIMBIRSKY, VALENTINE ALEXANDROVICH

(b. 1897)

Smirnov-Simbirsky comes of a poor family from the province of Simbirsk. His father died when the boy was five years old. His childhood was spent in dire poverty. In 1904 he completed a course in a vocational school. Later he worked in the city of Orenburg as a locksmith. From 1917 to 1922 he was employed in various iron works and foundries.

His first attempts at writing were made at the age of twelve. A volume of his poems was published in 1922.

THE SONG OF THE RED

We shall not fag! We shall not lag!
Our motto is forward!
Not for nothing we are known
As the nation of workmen.
  What are to us a fleeting grief,
  Hunger and need;
  By labor's might
  We shall conquer all in this life.
There were days when
Everywhere chaos reigned;
In a confused heap there lay
All kinds of rubbish and remains.

Everywhere the mute jaws
Of bare walls arose.
But under our control
Such things will never chance.
We have no fear
For such ruins in life:
We are strong with a united spirit,
With a creative mind.
Our workingmen's thought burns
With the knowledge of labor,
We, the great architects, the creators,
Fear no disasters.
In our hearts is no indecision,
Our gaze is clear, so is our reason.
Before us are our native fields,
And the blue space and heaven.
Understand and fearlessly go;
With a heavy blow strike down the want,
It is true, for us it is hard, but what of it,
Ahead of us it is brighter.
We forge, plane, saw,
We smite misfortune's core.
We shall not falter! We shall not fag!
Our motto is—forward!

TARASOV, EVGENII NIKOLAEVICH

(b. 1882)

The two volumes of his works were published in 1906 and in 1919.

PRAISE TO DARING

We are tired of living in twilight!
We have awakened, arisen;
We have waited too long for the fight,
For the young life we are yearning.
Vanish impotent fear!
Steady look and heavy blow!
Show more of sacred daring!

We need many a stubborn hand,
That in our foundries and furnaces
The blind and black masses
Of metal like a stream may glitter;
More passion, more ardor!
Closer to the fire press your chest,
Then the metal will be tempered.

Lift your torches higher!
In men's souls ye kindle fire;
Err—but dare!
The chains of ages will pass,
Only that which is taken by force
Will live, and will be sacred,
Will be sacred for ever!

TIKHOMIROV, NIKIFOR SEMENOVICH

(b. 1888)

Tikhomirov is the son of a peasant, and a native of the province of Yaroslav. He attended the rural school. Later he read many books on religious topics, among them the lives of the saints, the Psalms, and the Bible. At the age of nineteen he came to St. Petersburg. From 1908 till 1914 he worked in various factories and foundries; lately he has been employed at an electrical plant.

He took to his pen in 1911. One volume of his verse was published in 1919.

THE FACTORY

There it is—mighty, menacing, drunken;
It flares with a bright red
Surpassing the sunset of crimson;
It looks proudly at the azure of heavens.

It scatters shiny coins
Of sparks that laugh with thunder,
And the sun turns pale before it:
Stately is the giant of steel.

Forward it stares with a gaze of fire
Into the dark night,
Martial armor is its pride:
With passionate breath it sings.

From boilers, from rumbling machines,
The walls groan, the steel leaps.
From the singing furnaces and bellows
Into the bright distance I will not go.

This thunder, smoke, and clang
Have swallowed me in their waves;
They fascinate me with their red tale,
Driving dreadful slavish fear away.

There it is, the stern and bold knight!
It has thrown up the shaggy smoke;
Sooty, its face like fire,
It blusters with a muffled roar.

WITH THE BUZZING LATHES

With the ceaselessly buzzing lathes
I sing the turbulent rhyme.
Under the blows of steel hammers
The golden strings sing and whine.

My bosom is full of passionate desires,
I hear music in the intoxicated tumult;
A wave of ringing sounds rises;
And, like wind in the plains, thought flies.

I have embraced all with my naked soul;
The song pours down 'midst the clangor of steel.
Beyond the high factory wall
There is much sorrow and dismal grief.

But, in love with the elastic metal,
The factory son knows not grief;
Below the rocky summits
Motley valleys are spread before him.

I shall go where no one has passed before,
Without fear, sure of my power;
I have broken my fright long ago,
I have tempered myself in the furnace of revolt.

Laugh, my song, with the dance of the lathes,
Link the golden chains;
I have heard the eagle's call,
The ardent song of the turbulent·ocean.

YURIN, MICHAIL

(b. 1894)

Yurin is an illegitimate child, of unknown parentage. His foster-father was an old peasant from the province of Samara. The boy grew up tending cattle in a village. In 1909 he came to the city of Pugachev, where he worked in a joiner's shop. In 1911 he went to Astrakhan and thence to the oil wells at Grozny. The following year he was employed there as a locksmith in a large factory. In 1918 he returned to the city of his youth, Pugachev. Being an illiterate, he attended the night classes for adults.

His first verse was written in 1919. One volume of his works was published in 1922.

I AM THE MILLIONS

I

I am versatile. I am the millions!
I tear off the veil from starry fate!
With an echoing sound I kiss the slopes
Of your rocky monsters, O flowery space.

Growth is everywhere, My sprouts
Are bathed in the waves of the iron age!
I am the son of the factory and of tardy pleasure;
An eternal enigma, to all I am—an answer.

With a foggy mist of passionate rhyme
The infant days I swaddle.
And proud with the awe of the singing battle
I set all hearts afire.

I am crude and coarse, like the dowlas,
I am gray like the grass of the playful plains,
I am the symbol of Truth, the courage of Labor,
I am heavy as stone, I whirl like dust.

I hasten to freedom, I am bathed in azure;
In smoke I sing the battle's tales;
I pass everywhere like a thunderstorm
Filled with the clamor of my prayers.

I shall enchant all the living with one passion,
I know the secrets of the gray past;
I have a message of my own;
Above the world I soar, like a master.

I shall embrace all the boundless mystery,
I shall cut the space with the thought of ages;
Ceaselessly I shall listen to the free;
I am the world's genius, I am life's reason.

WHO ARE WE?

We are the children of songs of the grassy steppes,
Our emerald is the bright dew on the fields;
In dusty hovels we blossomed forth,
Our wilful might was forged by Labor.

We are the factory's peal and drone,
The smile of young and bright dawns.
We are the fire-faced rays of the rising sun
Of revolutionary days—joyful, crimson.

We are daring. There is no limit to us,
We pierce with our sight mute space;
A youthful host—we boldly call to revolt
The living, red in muddy pools.

We are the embodiment of the coarsely-clad masses,
The seditious blood cells in people's veins;
We are omnipotent, boundless;
We sing the song for the new ages.

ZABELIN, IVAN SEMENOVICH

(b. 1882)

Zabelin is a native of the province of Voronezh. His father, a former serf, was a tailor. The boy went to the municipal elementary school and upon his graduation with honors, remained there as an assistant. Later he attended the Teachers' Seminary, from which he graduated in 1902.

At the age of twelve he wrote three lyrics in the Ukranian language. Some of his works were published in 1909, in the newspaper *Voronezhsky Telegraf*. His verse, short stories, and satirical tales are to be found in various papers and magazines.

POWER IS IN US

The song of bondage is at an end,
My back I shall not bend.
For equal lot and brotherhood,
Spare not your life, my friends.

Even though you live in hovels
And should die prematurely,
Rather part with your life
Than by a master's hand be guided.

I shall boldly sing my song
Of the freedom of strong hands,
It is not enough for you, my friend,
To stoop beneath the *bourgeois* yoke.

Man is the crown of creation;
Now we are all equal.
Let not the worm of doubt gnaw you;
Workman, believe! the power is in us.

We will stand like a firm wall;
Wretched coward, off the road!
Not a cheap bargain did we make
When we traded the night for the day.

INDEX OF AUTHORS AND POEMS

A Bitter Lot, 5
Across the first snow I ramble
    ...., 190
A drought...., 192
Again the crude cart...., 189
ALEXANDROVSKY, V., 95, 105,
    106, 159
ANDREYEV, L., 143
ARSKY, P., 113, 114, 138, 164
ARTAMONOV, M., 48, 167
At the Foundry, 212
At the Lathe, 252-254
Bay Nag, The, 241-242
BEDNY, D. (PRIDVOROV, E.), 98,
    100, 104, 173
BELY, A., 41, 64, 143
BERDNIKOV, Y., 106, 108, 146,
    169
BEZYMENSKY, A., 95, 171
Blacksmith, The, 200-202
BLOK, A., 41, 53, 54, 143
Blue-bloused Workmen, The,
    237-239
BOGDANOV, 84
BORISSOV, 36
BUKHARIN, N., 72, 73
Call of the Earth, The, 204
Calling to United Work, 257-
    258
CHEKHOV, A., 143
Collective Will, The, 165
Communists, The, 211-212
Comrade, 185-188, 272

Crimson Temple, The, 242-243
DEYEV-KHOMYAKOVSKY, G., 177
DORONIN, 148
DOSTOYEVSKY, F., 51, 143
DROZHIN, S., 8, 10, 11
DRUZHININ, P., 47, 49, 56, 58,
    180
DUDOROV, 49
ESSENIN, S., 13, 21, 23, 24, 34,
    35, 37, 38, 39, 41, 43, 46, 49,
    50, 51, 52, 54, 56, 59, 61, 62,
    63, 64, 65, 67, 76, 182
Earth Calls, The, 260-261
Factory, The, 239-240, 279
FET, A., 53
FILIPCHENKO, I., 78, 85, 99, 101,
    110, 115, 116, 119, 122, 138,
    193
Flowers of Revolt, The, 245
Flute of Industry, The, 255-256
FOMIN, S., 35, 40, 49, 54, 56,
    58, 59, 63, 64, 65, 203
Freedom, 236
From the October Cycle, 160
GASTEV, A., 85
GERASSIMOV, M., 85, 125, 127,
    139, 142, 206
GOGOL, N., 4, 50, 143
GOLIKOV, 49
GORKY, M., 10, 82, 83, 85, 86,
    94, 143
Great Russian, The, 23
GUTZEVICH, 143, 145

Heavenly Factory, The, 214
Home Again, 23
HOMYAKOV, A., 43, 53
Hymn of the Tombs, 271
I am the millions . . . ., 282
I believe, 184
I came to you . . . ., 232
I sing of the fields . . . ., 249
In a humble monk's cowl . . . .,
    191
In the Factory, 261
IONOV, I., 85, 108, 119, 120, 132,
    210
Iron, 207–208
Iron Messiah, The, 127, 216
IVANOV, 144
KAZIN, V., 213
KIRILLOV, V., 78, 85, 96, 97,
    107, 109, 122, 123, 130, 140,
    151, 215
KLUYEV, N., 15, 16, 19, 24, 27,
    32, 33, 34, 35, 36, 39, 40, 41,
    42, 49, 50, 60, 74, 220
KLYCHKOV, S., 22, 51, 57, 59,
    225
KOLTSOV, A., 2, 3, 4, 5, 6, 8, 9
KUZMICHEV, 14, 24, 25
KUZNETSOV, 112
KVASS, 243–244
Left March, The, 229–230
LENIN, V., 70, 71, 72, 117
LOGINOV, 112, 147, 148
MALASHKIN, S, 36, 99, 118, 150,
    226
MASHIROV, A. (SAMOBYTNIK),
    98, 265
Masses, The, 196–199
MAYAKOVSKY, V., 108, 229

MINSKY, N., 43
Morning Prayer, The, 250–252
MOROZOV, I., 46, 231
NECHAYEV, G., 97, 102, 235
NEKRASSOV, N., 7, 8
Never, 170
NIKITIN, I., 8, 9, 10, 11
O cities!, 149
O my dear fields . . . ., 188–189
OBRADOVICH, S., 95, 100, 117,
    123, 127, 237
October 25, 219
O Seditious, Fiery, Passionate
    Factory . . . ., 256–257
Oh Thou, My Darling Rus . . . .,
    190–191
On Our Post, 268
On That Night . . . ., 269–271
ORESHIN, P., 12, 13, 19, 20, 23,
    26, 27, 29, 31, 34, 35, 36, 37,
    38, 39, 43, 47, 57, 241
Past, The, 85
Peasants' March, The, 178–179
POMORSKY, A., 97, 114, 245
Power is in us . . . ., 285
Praise to Daring, 277
PRASKUNIN, M., 17, 19, 21, 248
PRIDVOROV, E. *See* BEDNY
Prologue, The, 162
RADIMOV, P., 56, 61, 66, 249
Raspberry West, The, 168
Red Song, The, 223–224
Revolution, The, 266–267, 274
Rus, 233–234
Russia, 267
SADOFIEV, I., 78, 98, 103, 109,
    110, 117, 120, 127, 128, 131,
    133, 136, 250

SAMOBYTNIK. *See* MASHIROV
SANNIKOV, G., 269
Saviour, The, 243
SEMENOVSKY, D., 109, 272
Shattered Ikon, 205
SHEVCHENKO, T., 6, 7, 8
SHIRYAVETS-ABRAMOV, A., 14
SHKULEV, F., 97, 273
SMIRNOV-SIMBIRSKY, V., 115, 275
SOLOGUB, F., 143
SOLOVIEV, V., 41, 42
Song of the Hammer, The, 166
Song of the Red, The, 275–276
Struggle, The, 161
Sun Festival, The, 194–195
SURIKOV, I., 1, 8, 10, 11
TARASSOV, E., 105, 277
The band plays . . . ., 226–228
The wilderness of native plain . . . ., 225
There are the bitter loam, and . . . ., 222
There is a vast country . . . ., 221
TIKHOMIROV, N., 128, 137, 278
Tiller, The, 181, 248
Today, 172
TOLSTOY, L., 3, 33, 127

To the City, 246
To the Future, 217
To the Revolt, 267–268
To Russia, 262–264
TRIFONOV, 84
TROTSKY, L., 35
TSAREV, 39
TSARKOV-VYSOKOVSKY, 15
TURGENEV, I., 3
TYUTCHEV, F., 53
VERHAEREN, 140
We, 218
We shall take all, 209
Whenever I gaze . . . ., 184–185
Who Are We? 283
Will, The, 265
With the Buzzing Lathes . . . ., 280
With What Joy Throbs . . . ., 258–259
Wolf's Peril, The, 183–184
Workman's Palace, The, 247
Workmen's Hymn, The, 174–176
YAROPOLOV, 45, 47
YURIN, M., 113, 281
ZABELIN, I., 284